WHAT ARE THEY SAYING ABOUT CHRISTIAN-JEWISH RELATIONS?

What Are They Saying About Christian-Jewish Relations?

by

John T. Pawlikowski

PAULIST PRESS
New York/Ramsey

Library of Congress
Catalog Card Number: 79-56135

ISBN: 0-8091-2239-1

Published by Paulist Press
Editorial Office: 1865 Broadway, New York, N.Y. 10023
Business Office: 545 Island Road, Ramsey, N.J. 07446

Printed and bound in the
United States of America

Contents

Preface   vii

1. The Deicide Charge
   and New Testament Anti-Semitism   1

2. Christian Theology
   and the Jewish Covenant   33

3. Jewish Views of Christianity   69

4. Jesus and the Pharisaic Tradition   93

5. Christian Theology
   and the Jewish Land Tradition   109

6. Theological Perspectives
   on the Nazi Holocaust   129

7. Final Reflections   143

Notes   147

Bibliography   157

69854

*Dedicated to my Servite colleagues
who have given me much encouragement
and personal support.*

Preface

More than a decade has now passed since the historic declaration *Nostra Aetate* by the II Vatican Council on the Church and the Jewish people created a new climate in the relations between Judaism and Christianity. In the intervening years many individual Christian denominations in the Protestant community and a good number of national and regional groups of Catholic bishops have issued additional statements which have built on the basic thrust outlined in *Nostra Aetate.* The Vatican itself released guidelines and suggestions for implementing the Vatican II declaration in January 1975. The complete texts of these various post-conciliar statements have been compiled by Helga Croner in a volume called *Stepping Stones To Further Jewish-Christian Relations.*[1]

Additionally, beginning in the late fifties and continuing through the conciliar period, major textbook studies by Protestants, Catholics and Jews, initiated by the American Jewish Committee, exposed serious stereotyping of other religious groups in their basic educational materials. These self-studies, done by professional researchers from each tradition at Yale Unversity (Protestant materials), at St. Louis University (American Catholic texts), at the "Pro Deo" University in Rome (for Italian materials), at Louvain University (for French language texts in Europe and Canada) and at Dropsie College (for Jewish materials) brought to light the specific interreligious perceptions that needed attention if the more generalized appeals in the various declarations were to have genuine impact. The results of these studies were communicated to the religious community at large through the publication of such volumes as the late Bernhard E. Olson's *Faith and Prejudice*,[2] Claire Huchet Bishop's *How Catholics Look at Jews*[3] and my own work *Catechetics and Prejudice*.[4]

The writings of individual Jewish and Christian scholars during this period have aided the process initiated by the declarations and the textbook studies. Works such as Fr. Edward Flannery's *The Anguish of the Jews*,[5] the five volumes of *The Bridge* edited by Msgr. John Oesterreicher,[6] Jules Isaac's *The Teaching of Contempt*,[7] Rosemary Ruether's *Faith and Fratricide*,[8] to name only a few, have seriously undercut much of the traditional thinking about the Jewish-Christian relationship. New perspectives on the relationship have been put forth by such dedicated participants in the ongoing dialogue as Eva Fleischner, Eugene Fisher, Krister Stendahl, Franklin Littell, Alice and Roy Eckardt, Gregory Baum, Marc Tanenbaum, Irving Greenberg, Samuel Sandmel, the Rainbow Group and Ecumenical Theological Research Fraternity in Israel, Abraham Heschel and others. Some major biblical and systematic theologians in contemporary Christianity have also recently begun to address the question of the link between the two faith traditions. Jurgen Moltmann, E.P. Sanders, Edward Schillebeeckx, Hans Kung, and Paul Van Buren are a few such names. It now appears that after a decade of persistent efforts by a few theological pioneers a serious re-examination of the role of Judaism in Christian thought is finally beginning to penetrate the mainstream of theological investigation in the churches. The situation on the Jewish side is not quite as advanced although, especially among some Israeli scholars, there are a few initial explorations of how Christianity might be understood in a new light by Judaism.

Yet, despite the evident progress since Vatican II, it has become fashionable in some circles to proclaim that the Jewish/Christian dialogue is dead, that it started out with a great deal of euphoria in the era of Pope John XXIII and the Council but has not come to a screeching halt as a result of clashes over such core issues as peace and security in the Middle East, proselytizing and opposition to discussion of theological questions. As a person closely connected with the dialogue process during the greater portion of this period, I would be the first to admit that a lot of the early enthusiasm has evaporated and that many current points of tension have arisen. But I would just as strongly contradict any claim that the dialogue is dead. In retrospect it is good that some of the initial euphoria has vanished. While it proved useful as a prod for breaking the barriers that separated Jews and Christians for so long a time, it tended to push all controversial questions to the background. Ultimately such a situation would not prove productive for mutual understanding and respect. The dialogue will not reach maturity until Christians and Jews are able to candidly discuss their differences on all levels and genuinely profit from a grasp of the unique elements in each other's tradition.

From a national and international vantage point one must say that there has been a slow but steady increase in Christian study of Judaism and in Christian-Jewish conversation, especially on the grass roots level. The new interest in the Nazi holocaust which has produced more than twenty major conferences in the United States the last several years has greatly assisted this process. New dialogues are springing up in places which have never seen them before. Without hesitation, I would assert that more substantial conversation is taking place now than at any other period since II Vatican. Granted it is no longer headline news as it was in the sixties. The ongoing conflict in the Middle East has caused hard feelings on both sides. Yet, acknowledging this, it would be factually incorrect to say that the dialogue has ended. I would prefer to characterize the current atmosphere as one marked by normal growing pains. A rabbinic colleague remarked to me recently that in the last decade Jews and Christians have moved, as a result of their new encounter, from the status of second cousins to first cousins. Whether a further rapprochment will prove possible only time will tell. But the seeds for further development have definitely been sown during the period since II Vatican.

Accepting the thesis that the dialogue has a significant future, it is important to spell out where the two faith communities have come thus far in their encounter and what issues need to be confronted in the years ahead. What follows is an attempt to delineate the major issues and how various Christians and Jews are presently looking at them. In a work of this size it is impossible to present all perspectives and to treat all relevant questions. But there is little doubt that the topics covered in the following pages will remain central to any authentic dialogue for the foreseeable future.

John T. Pawlikowski, O.S.M.
Catholic Theological Union
Chicago Cluster of Theological Schools
February 1979

1
The Deicide Charge and New Testament Anti-Semitism

Probably no other accusation against the Jewish community by the Christian church is responsible for more Jewish suffering throughout history than the deicide charge, the verdict that the Jews of Jesus' time, in their blindness, put to death the very Son of God. This accusation laid the groundwork for a highly developed theology within Christianity which claimed that Jews, for the remainder of human history, were to be subjected to continual suffering and to live in a state of perpetual wandering without a homeland as a punishment for their grave sinfulness in killing Christ. This distorted Christian theology of Judaism was not simply a product of the ancient and medieval Christian mind but persisted well into our own era. Dr. Charlotte Klein of Frankfurt University has shown, for example, that when the first talk of a national homeland for Jews arose at the end of the last century the Catholic Church opposed the idea on the basis of the longstanding perpetual wandering theology. Dr. Klein offers two quotations from the authoritative, semi-

1

official Roman periodical *Civiltà Cattolica*.[9] The first
comes from an article written in 1897, the year of the first
Zionist Congress; the second is a quote from Pope Pius
X's reply to Theodore Herzl, the father of modern Zionism, on the occasion of his visit to the Vatican in January
of 1904:

(1)
1827 years have passed since the prediction of
Jesus of Nazareth was fulfilled, namely, that Jerusalem would be destroyed . . . that the Jews
would be led away to be slaves among all the
nations and that they would remain in the dis-
persion until the end of the world.

(2)
We are unable to favor this movement. We cannot prevent the Jews from going to Jerusalem—
but we could never sanction it. The ground of
Jerusalem has been sanctified by the life of Jesus Christ. As head of the Church I cannot answer you otherwise. The Jews have not recognized our Lord. Therefore we cannot recognize
the Jewish people.

The deicide issue was the major point of discussion
during the deliberations at the II Vatican Council on the
scheme dealing with the Church's attitude toward the
Jewish people. While the version finally approved by the
Council eliminated the specific condemnation of the historic deicide accusation (much to the disappointment of
many Jews and Christians), the conciliar decree *Nostra
Aetate* makes it quite clear that any collective accusation

against the Jewish community then or now for the death
of Jesus is contrary to Christian teaching:

> . . . what happened in his (i.e., Jesus') cannot be
> charged against all the Jews, without distinc-
> tion, then alive, nor against the Jews of today.
> . . . . the Jews should not be presented as reject-
> ed or accursed by God, as if this followed from
> the Holy Scriptures.[10]

Statements in a similar vein have come forth from a
number of official Protestant sources as well. A National
Council of Churches declaration issued in 1964 stated
that "especially reprehensible are the notions that Jews,
rather than all mankind, are responsible for the death of
Jesus the Christ, and that God has for this reason rejected his covenant people."[11] And the House of Bishops of
the Episcopal Church, meeting in St. Louis that same
year, spoke the following to all members of their commu-
nion:

> The charge of deicide against the Jews is a trag-
> ic misunderstanding of the inner significance of
> the crucifixion. To be sure, Jesus was crucified
> by *some* soldiers at the instigation of *some* Jews.
> But, this cannot be construed as imputing cor-
> porate guilt to every Jew in Jesus' day, much
> less the Jewish people in subsequent genera-
> tions. Simple justice alone proclaims the charge
> of a corporate or inherited curse on the Jewish
> people to be false.[12]

It is clear from the above statements, and many like
them, plus the updated research on textbooks provided

by Gerald Strober[13] for the Protestant community and by
Eugene Fisher[14] for the Catholic scene, that the Christian
churches have moved a long way toward complete elimination of the deicide charge from their teaching. This
without doubt must be seen as the greatest single achievement stemming from the decrees of II Vatican and other
church bodies and the textbook research produced over
the last decade. This does not mean, nonetheless, that the
accusation is part of a legacy that is now history. For the
more traditional beliefs regarding responsibility for the
crucifixion of Jesus continue to linger in popular culture
and piety.

New Testament scholars are virtually unanimous in
agreeing that the death of Jesus was viewed by the Roman government as a political execution. While there
may well have been some collaboration by the priestly
elite of the Jerusalem Temple in this execution (a group
of people incidentally who were roundly condemned in
Jewish materials from the period for the exploitation of
their own people), the primary responsibility is now
placed squarely on the shoulders of the imperial authorities by the vast majority of reputable exegetes. The
prominent New Testament scholar Oscar Cullmann
makes this point clear in his study on Jesus' relationship
to the revolutionary movements of his time. From his in-
vestigations Cullmann has concluded that Jesus was a
prisoner of the Romans, arrested by a cohort in the Garden of Gethsemane on Pilate's orders. The actual trial of
Jesus was conducted by Pilate and hence was a political
trial. Cullmann concludes that

> Thus Jesus suffered the *Roman* death penalty,
> crucifixion, and the inscription, the "titulus,"
> above the cross named as his crime the Zealotist

attempt of having strived for kingly rule in Israel, a country still administered by the Romans.[15]

Christian educational materials have for the most part utilized this scholarly perspective in their presentations. Nevertheless Dr. Eugene Fisher, executive secretary of the American Bishops' Secretariat for Catholic-Jewish Relations, feels some problems remain with the manner in which the crucifixion narrative is related by some Catholic materials. Despite the fact that the crucifixion story scored one of the highest positive ratings in the area of Christian-Jewish themes in Fisher's analysis, he still found a tendency to be unnecessarily vivid in describing the agonies of Jesus and to link "the people," "the Jews," or "the leaders of the people" with the events of Passion Week in a way that plays down the demonstrated guilt of Pilate and Rome which scholars such as Oscar Cullmann have revealed.[16]

Other difficulties remain on the popular level as well. An influential cultural creation such as *Jesus Christ Superstar*, seen by millions of Christians and perhaps more influential on their thinking than a hundred new textbooks, has the Jewish crowd shout "Crucify him, crucify him" over and over again. And a whole series of passion plays take place each year which continue many of the old stereotypes. The tendency, especially in certain sectors of Roman Catholicism, to dramatize the Holy Week liturgy, particularly on Good Friday, has added a new potential problem that needs close watching. Christians must avoid thinking that the various church declarations and educational changes have wiped out all traces of the deicide accusation.

We still have not attained the situation where the

Christian community at large clearly understands that a large portion of the Jewish population of Jesus' time would have endorsed at least in spirit his struggles against the Roman government and the corrupt Temple authorities. Most Christians still view the situation as Jesus and themselves over against the Jews when they read the passion narratives. In actual fact Jesus and his followers stood in concert with the large majority of the Jews of the period in opposing the Romans and the oppressive priestly elite. The passion story, apart from its later theological interpretations, should in fact serve as a source of unity between Jews and Christians, not as a source of the division and hostility we have witnessed for centuries. The Jewish historian Ellis Rivkin has made this point as well as anyone. Rivkin says that the question of "Who crucified Jesus?" needs to be rephrased as "What crucified Jesus?" As he sees it, Jesus died a victim of Roman imperial policy, of a type of regime "which, throughout history, is forever crucifying those who would bring human freedom, insight, or a new way of looking at man's relationship to man." If any Jews collaborated with the Romans in this venture, then they too deserve condemnation. The masses of Jews, however, who felt so stifled under Roman domination that they were to stage an outright revolt against its tyrannical authority a few years hence, cannot be blamed for the death of Jesus. Rather, insists Rivkin,

> In the crucifixion, their own plight of helplessness, humiliation and subjection was clearly written on the cross itself. By nailing to the cross one who claimed to be the messiah to free human beings, Rome and its collaborators indicated their attitude toward human freedom.[17]

It is such a framework that remains absent from a *Jesus Christ Superstar*, from most Christian textbooks and from contemporary Christian liturgy and preaching. The deicide charge will not finally be laid to rest until such a perspective becomes widespread among Christians. The problem is, however, that such a perspective is not easily developed from a simple reliance on the gospel texts dealing with the crucifixion and death of Jesus. Utilization of additional background material from modern scholarship on the Second Temple period is vital if the historical situation is ever to be understood as it actually was.

Connected with the inability to interpret properly the New Testament accounts of the trial and death of Jesus minus background material beyond the actual biblical text leads into a more fundamental issue: is the New Testament itself "anti-Semitic" in the way it portrays Jesus' relationship to the Jews? Several contemporary authors have taken up this question over the last decade or so. Gregory Baum, Bruce Vawter, Jules Isaac, Paul Kirsch and Joseph Grassi are only a few of the names. The most provocative challenge to usual Christian thinking on this question appears in Rosemary Ruether's controversial volume *Faith and Fratricide: The Theological Roots of Anti-Semitism.*[18] Her contention is that the Christologies developed by the New Testament to interpret the meaning of Jesus' suffering and death are in fact anti-Judaic at their core. This is especially the case with John. For Ruether, to use an oft-quoted phrase of hers, "anti-Judaism is the left hand of Christology."

Before proceeding to examine Ruether's claims in further detail it would be useful to look at the general approach of earlier Christian scholars who have dealt with the topic. While differing on some specific points, the vast majority of pre-Ruether discussions of the subject of

New Testament anti-Semitism wound up concluding that
there existed no anti-Semitism in the gospels or epistles.
Rather the opposition toward the Jews was due primarily
to five factors: (1) concrete hostility between Jews and
Christians in their early battle for converts; (2) to fear of
the Roman authorities which tended to downplay imperial responsibility for the death of Jesus at the expense of
Jewish culpability; (3) to a total misunderstanding of the
so-called "Judaizers" denounced in the later Pauline epistles such as Galatians; (4) to a failure on the part of the
later Christian community to understand many of the
supposedly anti-Jewish passages as a continuation of Jewish prophetic language intended primarily for members of
the church rather than as a judgment upon Judaism; and
(5) to disputes about Jewish law that were raging within
Judaism itself at the time of the church's birth.

Gregory Baum's volume *Is The New Testament
Anti-Semitic?*[19] typifies the usual Christian approach. Its
general conclusion was that any anti-Jewish trends to be
found in Christian history were the product of post-bibli-
cal thinking, in no direct way occasioned by the teaching
of the New Testament itself. Baum basically explained
any seemingly hostile passages toward Jews and Judaism
in the New Testament according to three principles. In
the first place, there were passages addressed specifically
to the Jewish community at Jerusalem of which Jesus
himself was a part. The Jews addressed here were the un-
faithful members of the community. They had ignored
Jesus' preaching and hence found themselves under divine judgment. It was only later generations of misguided
Christians who extended these condemnations to the
Jewish people at large throughout the centuries.

Baum's second principle of interpretation argued
that many of the statements by the New Testament writ-

ers that attributed blindness and hardness of heart to the Jews should be classed as prophetic declarations made by Christians belonging to the people Israel in the hopes of touching the hearts of their fellow Jews and converting them to the Christian faith. In this perspective such derogatory passages were not meant to describe first-century Judaism in its entirety. Rather they should be viewed as exhortatory sermons, in part prophetic and in part polemical, spoken by people who still looked upon themselves as members of the people Israel and whose aim was to try to lead their brothers and sisters to acceptance of the gospel message. Such passages, Baum maintains, acquired their anti-Semitic overtones only when they fell into the hands of gentile Christians who used them to judge Jewish religion as a whole.

Thirdly, Baum proposed that many sections of the New Testament which present a negative portrait of the scribes and Pharisees as well as the other opponents of Jesus had no intention of offering an historically accurate account of these groups. They aimed rather at exposing the deformations and pathologies which threaten religious expression in all ages and at initiating the Christian church itself into a spirit of critical self-examination. Jesus' conflict with various Jewish factions in his own time became symbolic for the New Testament writers of the perpetual conflict between authentic and inauthentic religion within Christianity. It was the unwillingness on the part of Christians to acknowledge this and to arrive at critical self-knowledge that led to the projection of this criticism onto the entire Jewish community. In so doing the church attempted to avoid the judgment of the Gospel on its own life and practice.

In a subsequent essay, his introduction to Rosemary Ruether's *Faith and Fratricide,* Baum rejects his earlier defense of the New Testament regarding the roots of anti-Semitism. We shall return to his present viewpoint later on in this chapter.

The rather classical defense of the epistles and gospels offered by Baum in *Is The New Testament Anti-Semitic?* is repeated in large measure by the respected Scripture scholar Fr. Bruce Vawter, C.M. In order to properly interpret the New Testament on the question of anti-Semitism Vawter insists we must begin with the assumption that the gospels and epistles had a fundamentally polemical goal. Hence they tend often to be over-simplified, onesided, easily misunderstood writings. Historically, Vawter sees the following factors as having contributed to the tone of the New Testament with respect to Jews and Judaism: (1) Jewish hostility toward the new Christian community of the first century, which was part of a mutual enmity; (2) the tendency of the biblical authors to write in absolute terms. This is the case with some of the references to "the Jews." They become, particularly in John, representatives of the unbelieving generation which confronted Jesus and the early church; and (3) the apocalyptic tone of New Testament thought which pitted the forces of good against the powers of evil in uncompromising language which condemns without qualification all those who refused to accept Jesus' message (new Israel versus old Israel).

Vawter thus recognizes a certain unquestionable hostility toward Jews in the New Testament. But it was only later Christian generations, reading the epistles and gospels uncritically, who constructed the popular forms of Christian anti-Semitism that were never intended by the New Testament writers. As Vawter sees it, the gospels did not represent Jesus as rejected by the Jews of his time nor as handed over by them to the Roman authorities for execution. "On the contrary," he says, "without exception they record his enormous popularity with 'the people' or 'the crowds' both in Galilee and in Judea, and they portray the circumstances of the crucifixion as precipitated by a small and desperate cabal of men who had to do their work covertly for fear of arousing against themselves a general rebellion of their own people. The anti-Jewish hostility of the Gospels, in other words, is selective."[20]

Vawter seconds the position of Oscar Cullmann regarding primary Roman responsibility for the execution of Jesus. While he feels that there was complicity in this act by certain members of the Sadducean priestly elite from the Jerusalem Temple, he points to the evaluation of this group offered by the noted Jewish historian Heinrich Graetz who described the Temple as having been directed at that time by men whose chief hallmarks were avarice and greed for power.[21] Vawter likewise is of the opinion that Jewish responsibility for the death of Jesus has been heightened by some of the gospel writers at the expense of Roman culpability in order to lessen the threat of imperial harassment of the early Christian community. In particular, Vawter insists, the image of Pontius Pilate has been cleaned up in Matthew, Mark and Luke based on what we know about him from other historical sources. The lone exception to this trend is the gospel of John where Pilate is definitely grouped with the evil and unbelieving multitudes who shun the truth of the gospel.

Another explanation of supposed New Testament anti-Semitism which follows the lines laid out above comes from the prominent Johannine scholar Raymond Brown in his earlier writings. In his introduction to the Anchor Bible translation of the fourth gospel Fr. Brown discusses

the evangelist's use of the term "the Jews" which has
been frequently pointed to as an example of gospel anti-
Semitism. His research shows that John employs this
term some seventy times in his gospel. Yet, says Brown,
in only a few instances is the term used as a designation
for the real, historical Jewish community of the period.
In great part John uses "the Jews" as a technical title. It
symbolizes all those people who are opposed to the teaching of Jesus and refuse to accept him as Lord. And in
view of the context in which Brown understands the
fourth gospel to have been written, he interprets this as
referring to those men and women who opposed Christianity in the late first century wherever they might have
lived:

> It is quite clear that in many instances the term
> "the Jews" has nothing to do with ethnic, geo-
> graphical, or religious differentiation. People
> who are ethnically, religiously and even geo-
> graphically Jews . . . are distinguished from the
> Jews. For instance, in John 9:22 the parents of
> the blind man, obviously Jews themselves, are
> said to "fear the Jews."[22]

Thus, as analyzed by Brown, "the Jews" in John constitutes a theological category, symbolizing any person,
Christian or non-Christian, Jewish or pagan, who would
reject with full knowledge the news of salvation through
Christ. In sum, Brown states without equivocation his
overall assessment of John: "John is not anti-Semitic; the
evangelist is condemning not race or people but opposition to Jesus."[23]

We will see later on that like Gregory Baum (though
not quite so explicitly) Fr. Brown has modified his view

about the anti-Semitic factor in John. Before that, however, it will be useful to look briefly at explanations regarding Pauline attitudes toward the Jewish people since up till now we have focused almost exclusively on the gospel accounts about Jesus. On one hand, an epistle like Romans is frequently appealed to by those advocating improved Christian-Jewish relations today as a good starting-point for a new Christian theology of the synagogue. On the other hand, many of Paul's remarks about the Torah seem to some to bespeak a deep hostility to Jewish law that serves as the very basis for the traditional contrast between Judaism and Christianity as religions of law and love respectively. And the almost at times vitriolic denunciations of the so-called "Judaizers" in Galatians further complicate the image of the Pauline school regarding Judaism.

Several Christian exegetes who have been active in the Christian-Jewish dialogue have come to the defense of the Pauline writings on the question of their anti-Semitic bias. Markus Barth feels that much of the blame for unwarranted distortions of Judaism supposedly developed out of teachings found in the epistle is in fact due to inaccurate interpretations of the Pauline message by later scholars. These Pauline interpreters depicted him as a rugged individualist who opted for a religion of mystical experience, ethical quietism, psychic introversion and almost satanic overestimation of sin in resolute oppositon to a Jewish or Judaeo-Christian religion of tradition, discipline, group responsibility and ethical commitment. Barth insists that such an outlook on Paul is no longer tenable. Paul did not merely abandon priestly sacrifice and circumcision. Rather he magnified both by showing what good resulted for all men and women by the one sacrifice made on the cross. Not the destruction but the renewal of the Israel of God was his goal. "Just as Moses offered his life to God," says Barth, "to make, if possible, atonement for his people," so Paul writes, "For I could wish that I myself were accursed and cut off from Christ for the sake of my brethren, my kinsmen by race" (Exodus 32:32; Romans 9:3).[24] A man who writes in this fashion, Barth maintains, can hardly be termed an anti-Semite.

Barth believes that Paul needs to be seen as standing in the tradition of the biblical prophets who frequently had to speak harsh and challenging words to their own people. But this does not prove that Paul hated or despised Jews any more than Jeremiah could be so described:

> When Paul posits a spiritual temple as over against the building of stone; when he calls for circumcision of the heart, not of the flesh only; when he puts righteousness and love, brotherliness and humility, full obedience and faith above all virtues and accomplishments claimed by some of his contemporaries, then he wages a typically Jewish war.[25]

According to Barth's understanding of Pauline thought, Israel continues to give honor and glory to God even after the resurrection of Christ. Israel's task remains to give witness to God's existence, covenant, and blessing among the Gentiles. Paul sees a continuing Jewish mission to the nations. And for that reason, Barth insists that any Christian attempts to proselytize Jews are repugnant to the very heart of the Pauline message. For Barth the full idea of salvation in the Pauline body of literature still retains its basic Jewish social character. Salvation is something that will be realized at the end of history when church and synagogue are finally reconciled.[26]

With respect to the problem of the people usually referred to as "Judaizers" in the epistle to the Galatians, Barth makes the point that they were most likely not born Jews but Gentile-Christians. Otherwise they would not have isolated circumcision from the other 612 commandments of the Torah and considered it a substitute for observing the entire Law. Also, if they had been Jewish Christians, they would have been circumcised at birth. But Galatians indicates that they were only in the process of accepting circumcision. Paul's venom is thus directed against ritualistic, pagan-born distorters of the gospel message, not against Jews or Jewish Christians. His condemnation of them sprang as much from his own "liberal" understanding of Judaism as from his acceptance of the teachings of Jesus. Paul's line of argument in this regard parallels to some degree the rabbinic teaching of the period which held, for example, that the Adamite and Noahite commandments need not be fully imposed upon Gentiles for them to attain participation in the coming final kingdom.

Barth warns, as a result of his research into the question of the opponents of the Pauline message in Galatians, that it is misleading to call them "Judaizers." It conveys an anti-Semitic ring and suggests that Jewish-born Christians were forcing upon free Gentile Christians some unnecessary or even harmful components of their Jewish heritage. This simply was not the case.

Another New Testament scholar who has looked extensively at the question of the Jews in Pauline theology is Krister Stendahl. In an essay that has now become somewhat of a classic, Stendahl argues in a vein that is similar to Barth. He believes that what he terms a

"Western introspective mentality" has been imposed on the writings of Paul by his interpreters in Western Christianity, especially those coming from the Protestant community. Stendahl is convinced that such interpretations of Paul have fundamentally disfigured Paul's real teaching and intensified the Jewish-Christian problem:

> . . . Paul's statements about "justification by faith" have been hailed as the answer to the problem which faces the ruthlessly honest man in his practice of introspection. Especially in Protestant Christianity—which, however, at this point has its roots in Augustine and in the piety of the Middle Ages—the Pauline awareness of sin has been interpreted in the light of Luther's struggle with his conscience. But it is exactly at that point that we can discern the most drastic difference between Luther and Paul between the sixteenth and the first century, and perhaps between Eastern and Western Christianity.[27]

Luther's struggle with his own conscience read in the framework of late medieval piety led him to interpret Pauline statements as answers to the quest for assurance about personal salvation out of a common human predicament. And Luther's own struggle became a model for the way many subsequent Christians conceived of the Pauline debate with the Jewish tradition. Paul however, according to Stendahl, was not concerned primarily with the personal struggle for salvation but with the possibility for Gentiles to be included in the messianic community.

With respect to the famous chapters in Romans in which Paul speaks theologically about the Jewish-Christian relationship, Stendahl is of the view that Paul here intended to attack head-on what he perceived were unwarranted superiority feelings on the part of Gentile Christians over against the people of Israel. The mysterious coexistence between Jews and Christians here developed by Paul is designed to counter the spiritually haughty attitude he picked up among Roman Christians. It may not be coincidental in Stendahl's eyes that for four pages in the Greek text (Romans 10:17 to the end of Chapter Eleven) we do not find even a single mention of Christ. And the doxology concluding this section is the only Pauline doxology that is not christological in theme. The emphasis here, Stendahl observes, is on "God language":

> Now if this language usage is conscious it is interesting; if it is unconscious it is even more interesting. Nobody could ever claim that Paul did not have the guts to wave the Christ flag, that he would fall short of evangelistic zeal and zest. Whatever flaws there are in the great apostle, this is not one of them. That is why this absence of Christ language, this changing of thinking into God language, is so striking. Paul is actually teaching a mysterious coexistence.[28]

In light of this understanding of Romans 9–11 it is impossible in Stendahl's judgment ever to accuse Paul of anti-Semitism. While he may have been guilty of minor indiscretions at times regarding Jews, his major theological reflection on the church's link with Judaism reveals a love and respect so profound that it completely wipes out the validity of any other comments he might have made during his missionary career.

Having looked at representative arguments for the claim that the New Testament is not basically anti-Semitic, we need now to look at the counter-arguments. As indicated earlier, probably no thesis advocating that the roots of traditional anti-Semitism lie in the New Testament itself has received as much attention as that of Rosemary Ruether. In *Faith and Fratricide* she tries to demonstrate that the term "Jews," as used in the gospels, Acts, and the Pauline writings, signifies the Jewish religious community. As a result the word "Jews" took on the role of a hostile symbol for all those men and women who dare to resist and reject the gospel teaching. She finds that the book of Acts utilizes the term in this hostile sense some forty-five times, while the term "a Jew," "Jews," or "Jewish" is applied to Christians on less than ten occasions. On the grounds of her extensive research Ruether has become convinced that

> Judaism, represented by its dominant religious consciousness, was hopelessly apostate and represented a heritage of apostasy which merited its rejection as the true guardian of the vineyard of Israel and the election of the Gentiles instead.[29]

She attributes this perspective not to Gentile converts, but to alienated and angry Jewish sectarians who were certain they possessed the true interpretation of the Scriptures and were the cornerstone of God's people, but experienced rejection and rebuff at every turn from the synagogue leadership.

Dr. Ruether also stresses the shifting of blame in the gospels for the deaths of Jesus and his disciples from the Roman political leadership to the Jewish religious authorities. The usual explanation for this, the need to avoid harassment from the Romans after the death of Jesus in order to carry on the mission to the Gentiles, does not prove convincing to her. She says that we should note the full nature of the shift. It was not merely from Roman to Jewish authority, but from *political* to *religious* authority. The gospel writers, in her view, felt it important to cast the blame for the deaths of Jesus and his disciples not merely upon the Jewish political hierarchy of the day, but specifically upon the head of the Jewish *religious* tradition and its authority. This leads us to believe that the reason for the shift did not arise simply from the desire to insure the success of the campaign for Gentile converts, but from the wish to engage in a polemic toward the Jewish religious tradition itself:

> The idea that the religious authority of "apostate Israel" has "always" killed the prophets, and, therefore, culminates its own heritage of apostasy by killing the great messianic prophet, totally governs the entire story line of all the Gospels.[30]

Ruether also takes issue with benign interpretations of St. Paul on the Jewish question. She is especially critical of those contemporary ecumenists who look positively toward Romans 9–11. They have the right intentions but are guilty of bad exegesis. As she sees it, the "mystery" relationship between Christians and Jews advocated by Paul in no way suggests an ongoing validity for the Jewish covenant as an instrument of salvation in its own right. Paul admits only one authentic covenant of salvation:

> For Paul, there is, and has always been, only
> one true covenant of salvation. This is the cov-
> enant of the promise, given *apart from the Law*,
> to Abraham and now manifest in those who be-
> lieve in Abraham's spiritual son, Christ. The
> people of the Mosaic covenant do not now and
> never have had any way of salvation through
> the Torah itself. God never intended to save his
> people through the Law.[31]

Paul recognized, says Ruether, that Jews would refuse to
enter this new community of Israel or accept it as the
spiritual lineage of the promise given to Abraham for the
foreseeable future. But this hardening of Jewish hearts
would ultimately change. God did not "cast off his people" in the sense that he intends to lead them into the
church at the end of time. For Ruether, then, the fact
that Paul proclaims the "mystery" of Israel does little to
allow a place for the ongoing authenticity of the Mosaic
covenant as such or to make room for any spiritual relation to God through Judaism. "In this sense," she says,
"he enunciates a doctrine of the rejection of the Jews (rejection of Judaism as the proper religious community of
God's people) in the most radical form, seeing it as rejected not only now, through the rejection of Christ, but
from the beginning."[32] The ultimate aim of Paul's "mystery" theology of Judaism is not to grant any permanent
validity to Judaism, but only to guarantee the ultimate
vindication of Christianity.

Even though she offers serious critiques of the synoptic gospels, Acts and Paul for their anti-Judaic orientation, Dr. Ruether reserves her strongest attack for the
gospel of John. In the fourth gospel, she maintains, the

"unbelief of the Jews" is related to a deep theological mystery. John depicts "the Jews" as the very incarnation of the false, apostate principle of the fallen world, alienated from its authentic existence in God. They typify the totally carnal person who knows nothing of the spiritual realm. They are totally time-bound in their existence, unable to recognize, like the spiritual brothers and sisters of Jesus, the *kairos* of the Christ Event (John 7:6). Their instinctive reaction to the revelation of the spiritual Son of God is to murder him, for they are aware that his coming has unmasked their false way of living: "In this murderousness they manifest their true principle of existence. They show that they are 'not of God, but of the Devil,' who was a liar and a murderer from the beginning. . . ."[33]

Ruether clearly divorces herself from those "apologists" in Christian circles who claim that the division John forges between the "sons of light" and "the sons of darkness" is mere allegory which the fourth gospel never meant to apply in a literal way to Christians and Jews. Her contention is that John turned a realistic inner spiritual conflict within humankind—the person in God versus the person alienated from God—into a division between two differing faith postures—Christianity and Judaism. In so doing John gave the ultimate theological form to the diabolizing of "the Jews" which served as the primary source of all future forms of anti-Semitism in Christian history. Hence the roots of the church's anti-Semitic tradition stretch back into the New Testament itself, to the Christology of John in particular. The Christian community, understanding the Scriptures Christologically, alone share in the life of the Father. The Jewish community, which interprets the Scriptures as a testimony to an ongoing covenant with Abraham and Moses, are "the children of the Devil" who have never known Christ or his Father. The remedy for anti-Semitism is crystal-clear for Ruether: "There is no way to rid Christianity of its anti-Judaism, which constantly takes social expression in anti-Semitism, without grappling finally with its Christological hermeneutic itself."[34]

As might be expected, Dr. Ruether's radical critique of the New Testament as the source of anti-Semitism has drawn several responses from Christian scholars. In the first place, she has persuaded Gregory Baum to draw away from the arguments he made in his volume discussed earlier. In an introductory essay in *Faith and Fratracide* he states unequivocally that Ruether's book has convinced him he must now change his mind on the subject of New Testament anti-Semitism. He now believes, after having examined Ruether's study, that Paul, for example, never had any intention whatsoever of acknowledging the Jewish religion as a way of grace. In the Pauline perspective Israel had gone blind. It now represented death and spiritual slavery. Yet God did not totally abandon the Jews. Their election remained, not as a source of grace in the present time, but as a divine promise of the eventual conversion of the Jews at the conclusion of human history and their absorption into Christianity, the one true Israel. Baum now writes:

> All attempts of Christian theologians to derive
> a most positive conclusion from Paul's teaching
> in Romans 9–11 (and I have done this as much
> as others) are grounded in wishful thinking.
> What Paul and the entire Christian tradition
> taught is unmistakably negative: the religion of
> Israel is now superseded, the Torah abrogated,
> the promises fulfilled in the Christian church,

the Jews struck with blindness, and whatever
remains of the election to Israel rests as a burden upon them in the present age.[35]

Baum insists that if the church is really serious about rid-
ding itself of the anti-Jewish bias built into its teaching, a
few marginal changes will not be sufficient. Rather what
is called for if the cleansing is to be meaningful is an examination and reinterpretation of the Christ Event itself.
Nothing less will do.

While not writing directly in response to Dr.
Ruether, the Christian scholar from Israel Fr. Joseph
Stiassny confirms at least some of her points regarding
the fourth gospel. He distinguishes sharply between comments against the Jews in the synoptic gospels and in
John. The former he views as essentially "in-house" comments, common to both the Jewish prophetic tradition
and to the warring parties within Second Temple Judaism. But by the time John comes along, the situation has
changed significantly. At the time of the final editing of
the fourth gospel, the church and the synagogue had become radically separate entities. Christianity's rupture
from Judaism had been finalized. Unlike Paul and the
synoptic writers, John's attitude toward the Jews is not
missionary but apologetic and polemical. It is intended to
counter Jewish propaganda and undergird Christian
claims. In Stiassny's eyes John employs the expression
"the Jews" to indicate that the Jewish people of his day
are the spiritual descendants of the Jewish authorities
who showed hostility to Jesus during his ministry. The
refusal of the Jews to believe becomes for John the symbol of all men and women everywhere who fail to accept
the message of the gospel.[36]

Fr. Raymond Brown has also seemingly modified

his position on no anti-Semitism in John which he articulated in the Anchor Bible. His change of viewpoint is nowhere near as dramatic as that of Gregory Baum. But there appears to be a significant switch in his thought as presented in an article in *"Worship"* magazine in 1975. Brown now says that by deliberating using the term "the Jews" where other gospel writers refer to the Jewish authorities or various Second Temple Jewish parties John means to extend to the synagogue of his own day the blame that an earlier tradition had pinned on the authorities. While John was not the first to engage in such extension, he is the most insistent New Testament author in this regard. Brown explains this process in John as owing to the persecution Christians were experiencing in his time from the synagogue authorities. Jews who professed Jesus to be the Messiah had now been officially expelled from Judaism, thus making them vulnerable to Roman investigation and punishment. Jews were tolerated by Rome; but who were these Christians whom the Jews disclaimed?

Brown goes on to say that this teaching of John about the Jews which resulted from historical conflict between church and synagogue in his day can no longer be taught as authentic doctrine by contemporary Christianity. Christians today must come to see that such teachings, while a realistic part of our biblical heritage, are no longer valid belief. He definitely feels a more radical solution is needed for the anti-Judaic material in the fourth gospel than merely softening the translation to "Judeans" or "Judaists," or offering the explanation that John often uses the term "the Jews" when the context implies that the chief priests alone were the culprits. Though Brown would likely shy away from the radical theological surgery suggested by Ruether as a corrective for the New

Testament view of Jews and Judaism, he does advocate
the need for significant change. The problem is that he
stops short of any overall approach to the issue. He likewise fails to really deal with the radical implications of
the approach to biblical materials that he suggests in his
call to abandon much of the Johannine theology of Judaism.[37]

Negative reactions to *Faith and Fratricide* have
come from several Christians long associated with the
Jewish-Christian dialogue. Msgr. John Oesterreicher, one
of the dialogue's pioneers, of the Institute of Judaeo-
Christian Studies at Seton Hall University has taken
strong exception to the book. In an Institute paper titled
the *Anatomy of Contempt* he rejects Ruether's basic con-
tentions about the anti-Semitic roots in the epistles and
gospels and goes on to accuse her of undermining authentic Christian faith. He cites the Jewish scholar Leo
Baeck's much more sympathetic treatment of Paul on the
Jewish question. He criticizes her generally for a failure
to understand the rabbinic style of interpretation which
Oesterreicher feels had a great impact on the mode of
Pauline argumentation. With regard to her charge
against the fourth gospel he claims that no competent
New Testament scholar in the present day "thinks that
'the Jews' in St. John's gospel are the empirical Jews, the
historical Jewish community, the people in the villages
and towns of the land of Abraham and his descendants.
All sound interpreters agree that in the instances that
seem to degrade Jews, 'the Jews' is a theological cipher or
symbol for a world that denies itself to Jesus."[38]

Several other critics of Ruether's thesis are much
more sympathetic than Oesterreicher to the basic goals of
Faith and Fratricide. In a co-authored article Thomas A.
Idinopulos and Roy Brown Ward do not quarrel with

Ruether's proposition that the foundations for anti-Judaic thought were planted in the New Testament. Certainly, they argue, Matthew's gospel represents a genuine hardening of attitudes toward Jews articulated in such themes as the rejection of the "sons of the kingdom" (i.e., the Jews) whom God will cast into outer darkness. Likewise, they say that Ruether's views that John's gospel vilifies the Jews can hardly be contradicted. As they see it, John moves the "crime of the Jews" very close to what eventually takes shape as the deicide charge. But the appearance of certain forms of anti-Judaic thought in portions of the New Testament does not automatically justify the Ruetherian contention that anti-Judaism is of necessity the left hand of Christology.

Indinopulos and Ward are especially troubled by the position taken by Ruether with respect to Pauline theology. It is difficult for them to comprehend how she can arrive at the conclusion that in Paul Judaism is not an ongoing covenant of salvation in which authentic worship makes possible a genuine relationship with God. As they see Paul, he only characterizes Gentiles, not Jews, as those who "knew not God." In fact, Paul himself boasts of his Jewishness. He never argues that Judaism represents false worship of God, but only that a new righteousness has been revealed (Romans 1:17; 3:21; 10:3) which has brought about a new phase in this history of salvation. His adherence to this new revelation does not lead him to deny the holiness of the law (Romans 7:12) nor the election of the Jews (Romans 11:28). These authors find it difficult to understand how Paul can be considered any more anti-Judaic than other Jewish sectarian groups of the period such as Qumran who joined Paul in believing that something new was taking place in history under divine guidance. Unlike the Qumran sectarians who an-ticipated the destruction of mainstream Judaism (which they considered in a state of apostasy), Paul expressed hope for the ultimate salvation of all Israel (Romans 11:26).[39]

In an essay prepared for presentation at the 1978 American Academy of Religion meeting the Episcopalian New Testament scholar John T. Townsend acknowledges that Dr. Ruether's estimate of the anti-Jewish stance of the gospel of John reflects the opinion of most competent exegetes. Townsend points out several instances of this anti-Jewish bias in John. But he also says that there are good reasons to hold that the fourth gospel is not as anti-Jewish as frequently claimed. John does not hesitate, for example, to affirm the Jewish context of his narrative. He does not disguise the fact that Jesus himself was Jewish and has him, together with John the Baptist, addressed as Rabbi. John also makes good use of the Hebrew Scriptures, thereby affirming the important role of the people Israel in the divine plan of salvation. Even though certain sections of the Johannine passion narrative appear to heighten Jewish involvement in the crucifixion, at other points in the story John is less anti-Jewish than the other gospel writers. Whereas the synoptic gospels depict the charge against Jesus as blasphemy against Jewish religious beliefs, John 11:48 clearly indicates that the Jewish authorities were concerned that Jesus' teachings might harm political relations with imperial Rome. John also highlights Roman responsibility for the execution of Jesus in a way that is unique among the gospels.

Townsend admits that the most common basis for John's supposed anti-Judaism is his use of the term "the Jews." He feels that the case here has been overstated by Ruether and others. The designation "Jew" does not always appear in a negative way in John, though there are definitely any number of places where it does. Hence a nuanced approach to the Johannine use of the term "the Jews" is required. John, for example, reports that Jesus himself was a Jew and that Jews occupy a special place in the salvific plan of God. And while John generally gives the term "Jew" an unfavorable or neutral connotation, it is useful to note that his occasional use of the terms "Israel" and "Israelite" always convey a favorable tone.

Townsend insists, on the basis of his investigation, that the anti-Jewish prejudice in John, though real, does not appear as extreme as some maintain. It appears to him that this anti-Jewish bias entered the text of the fourth gospel at a relatively late stage in its composition. It likely comes from the period when the Johannine community no longer looked upon itself as part of the Jewish family. Very probably it reflects the concrete experience of the author and his community of having been expelled from the synagogue. This has led John to assume that Jesus and his disciples had endured parallel experiences among the Jews of their time. The end result of these later inclusions was a gospel "containing a strange mixture of some of the most anti-Jewish parts of the New Testament resting upon a relatively pro-Jewish Johannine tradition."[40]

Townsend's approach is thus similar to that of Fr. Brown's. He too implies that John was directing his assaults against real Jews of his time, even though these people had also acquired a symbolic value for his theology. He also feels that this theology cannot stand uncorrected as Christians articulate their attitudes toward Judaism today.

We have now seen several divergent approaches to the problem of New Testament anti-Semitism. All come from scholars highly conscious of the history of persecution of the Jewish people and keenly intent on terminating this history once and for all. Their lack of agreement, however, gives evidence that the issue will remain a hotly contested one for some time to come. No total resolution lies in sight. Nonetheless some tentative conclusions are possible. (1) It is clear that read with some sophistication the gospels present a case for basic Roman responsibility for the death of Jesus. On this point, Dr. Ruether's contention about the deliberate switching of blame to Jewish religious authorities is not that strong. There was some attempt to whitewash Roman guilt, at least in the snyoptics. But there is no clear evidence, contrary to Dr. Ruether, that the primary motivation here was theological rather than political. Hence, sufficient background information should provide the Christian believer with a fairly accurate understanding of the situation. The problem remains, however, with how this background information is to be made available. So many Christians read the gospels without such information. How are they to come to know what Fr. Brown insists they should know, namely that the literal teaching of the New Testament about Judaism cannot be taken at face value as the basis for a contemporary theological approach? This is an issue that the churches have not yet squarely addressed.

(2) Ruether probably overexaggerates Pauline anti-Judaism. He shows a greater love and respect for the continuing validity of Jewish religious expression that she is willing to admit. Nonetheless, I think she and Gregory Baum are right when they criticize the overuse of Romans 9–11. This section of the epistle ends on a conversionalist note that I personally find unacceptable today in the light of what we have come to know about Judaism and in virtue of the Jewish experience of the Nazi holocaust. Stendahl is too optimistic in his interpretation of Paul's intention

here. What we can say is that Romans 9–11 undercuts any attempt by Christians to totally invalidate the meaningfulness and beauty of the Jewish religious covenant. But we cannot stop here. We need to build a new theology of Judaism which will pick up Paul's struggle with the question, but go well beyond him on the basis of resources he never knew.

(3) There appears to be a growing consensus among recent Johannine studies, in direct refutation of Oesterreicher, that the fourth gospel does intend to condemn the specific Jewish community of its day. While it is true that the actions of this concrete, historical community become a symbol for unbelief anywhere, we cannot simply assert that John in no way had the Jews of his time in mind when he penned his critique. The issue of the anti-Semitism of John is far from a settled question. It poses problems that the more internal Jewish battles found in the other gospels do not. I am convinced it is possible to present the Johannine Christology without of necessity denigrating Judaism as such. But this will still take much study and reflection by scholars. There is also present here the same problem alluded to with reference to the account of the crucifixion. How is the ordinary Christian man or woman to know that the negative references to Jews should be interpreted in an historical context and not globally?

(4) The denunciation of the Pharisees, so common to the synoptic gospels, is an issue on which Dr. Ruether's research shows some definite weakness. This is surprising in view of the fact that she has shown awareness of the new research on the Pharisees in other of her writings.[41] A considerable part of the hostility toward the Pharisees in the New Testament may in fact be explained by inter-Pharisaic contestation. Ruether gives too little due to this

possibility in *Faith and Fratricide*. We shall return to the question of Jesus and the Pharisees in Chapter Four.

(5) The attacks against the so-called "Judaizers" can be disposed of rather easily. These people were simply not representative of the Jewish mainstream. Many Jews of the time would have objected to their rigidity in Torah interpretation as strongly as did Paul. It is also likely that they were not even Jewish by birth. Yet when these passages are read without explanation the average Christian may take them as condemnations of Judaism as a whole. Here again we meet head-on the problem of background material that remains unsolved on the popular level.

2
Christian Theology and the Jewish Covenant

Both the Yale and St. Louis University studies on Christian textbooks showed serious distortion of Judaism on the question of the continuing value of the Jewish covenant. Without question some progress has been made since, and because of, these studies. The easy stereotyping of the Jewish covenant as having been simply fulfilled by the Christian covenant, the notion that Judaism was a religion based in legalism while Christianity was a religion rooted in love, and the idea that Judaism lost its reason-for-being with the coming of Christ have been modified to some extent as a result of recent scholarship. There has been an increasingly clear acknowledgement by Christians that Judaism retains a value in its own right after the coming of the Christian church and that the religious spirit of the Hebrew Scriptures is permeated by loving kindness rather than by legalistic strictures. There is also a growing awareness of the deep contribution that the reformist elements in Second Temple Judaism made to the thinking and lifestyle of Jesus and early Christianity. And the 1975 Vatican Guidelines on Catholic-Jewish relations clearly urged Christians to come to understand Jews as *they define themselves*, not as the church might imagine them to be. Gone are the days when Christian apologists could simply shoot down the beliefs of straw-Jews created by the Christian imagination.

But a serious problem still remains in this area despite the improvements since II Vatican and the textbook research. It likely will continue for some time. The reason is that in dealing with the relationship between the two faith traditions we are touching upon a central nerve of Christianity. Its basic self-definition is at stake. Coming to grips with this issue will not prove easy as a result, for we are dealing with creedal statements couched in a vocabulary of the "New Moses," the "new Covenant," "the new Israel," and "the New Jerusalem," that have been central to Christian theology since its inception.

Several present-day biblical scholars and theologians such as J. Coert Rylaarsdam, Monika Hellwig, Rosemary Ruether, Gregory Baum, A. Roy Eckardt, Paul Van Buren, Peter Chirico, James Parkes and E.P. Sanders have addressed the question.[42] The list becomes longer each year. In addition, some of the most prominent names in contemporary Christian systematic theology have begun for the first time to give serious attention to the place of Judaism in Christian theological formulation. Included here are Hans Kung, Edward Schillebeeckx, Wolfhart Pannenberg and Jurgen Moltmann.

The first group of scholars, all of whom have been closely connected with the ongoing Christian-Jewish encounter, have challenged in different ways the simplistic assertion of traditional Christian faith that the church fulfilled all that was of any value in Judaism. They have recognized that Christians must come to view the Jewish "no" to Jesus as a positive contribution to the ultimate salvation of humankind, not as merely an act of unfaithfulness or haughty blindness. The second group of systematicians, who have come to an examination of the question much later than the first group, generally are not as radical in their reassessment. But since these latter scholars are significantly responsible for the creation of much of contemporary Christian theology even a limited change of perspective on their part carries great potential significance.

We shall first examine a representative selection of view-points from those who have been intimately involved in Jewish-Christian discussions. They can basically be categorized into two groupings. The first wishes to re-incorporate Christianity into the original Jewish covenant. The second acknowledges two covenants that are different but complementary. Both schools of thought go well beyond the initial, pre-Vatican II explorations of the subject by an earlier generation of Christian theologians such as Jacques Maritain and Charles Journet who basically opted for a "mystery" approach to the ultimate Jewish-Christian relationship, following closely the line of argument developed by Paul in Romans 9–11.

A significant example of the single covenant theory can be found in the writings of Monika Hellwig. She believes that the simultaneous and complementary participation of Christianity and Judaism in the same covenant requires a restatement of some central concepts by the church. The most crucial of these is the traditional Christian assertion that the Messiah came in the person of Jesus of Nazareth and that those who recognized him were welcomed into his kingdom, while among his own people many refused to believe in him with the consequent punishment of being left in outer darkness. This, she strongly maintains, constitutes an oversimplification of the original stand of the apostolic community. A more accurate for-

mulation in her mind would be "that the cry of the early
Christian community, 'Jesus is Lord and Christ,' was and
remains a prophetic assertion by which Christians have
pledged themselves to a task of salvation yet to be accom-
plished. Even to the Christian there is a most important
sense in which Jesus is not yet Messiah."[43] In her eyes the
ultimate eschatological tension has not been resolved
through the Christ Event. Rather the Messianic Event
needs to be seen as "lengthy, complex, unfinished and
mysterious."

Dr. Hellwig feels that we must now speak of Jesus in
phenomenological terms. In such a perspective Jesus becomes the place of encounter of the human person with
the transcendent God, something Christians have experienced as central in all human existence. This experience,
though pivotal for authentic religious experience, is but
one aspect of the covenant God has made with Jews and
Christians. There are other central aspects of true religious experience that Jews continue to possess through
their ongoing encounter with the Father.

In a presentation to the 1977 American Academy of
Religion convention Professor Paul Van Buren began development of a thesis (which he hopes will eventuate in a
multi-volume work) which in some ways places him in
the single covenant school. Van Buren insists that the
church has an identity apart from Judaism, a divinely ap-
pointed identity. It is not merely one among several Jewish sects. The church is the community of the Gentiles
who have been drawn by the God of the Jews to worship
him and make his love known among the nations. Christianity's developing appreciation of Judaism in no way
implies a dilution of its affirmation of Jesus as the Christ.
Nor must the church stop confessing Jesus as Son of

God. According to Van Buren, the new revelation in Jesus was the manifestation of the divine will that Gentiles too are welcome to walk in God's way. For those Gentiles who through the Christ Event came for the first time to be drawn into the plan of God, what took place in Jesus could not be understood as merely one episode in the history of salvation. Rather it "marked a genuinely new beginning, a step out and beyond the circle of God's eternal covenant with his people, the Jews. But it surely cannot and does not detract from, much less annul, that covenant. . . .Indeed, this new move to the Gentiles was already implied in his covenant with Israel, for Israel has always worshiped the God of Israel as the King of the Universe."[44]

For Van Buren, then, Jesus is the Christ of the Church, but he is not the Jewish Messiah as Christians have traditionally claimed. While, in some ways, Van Buren might be better placed in the double covenant school, I have chosen to identify him with the single covenant group because of his great stress on the fact that God's Way is ultimately one. Judaism was exposed to that Way first of all. Then through the Jew Jesus of Nazareth the nations finally were allowed to experience the Way, though in a manner different from that of the Jews. This admission of the Gentiles into the Way was, however, always envisioned in the original revelation to Israel. Van Buren would thus appear to maintain that Judaism and Christianity are both valid and complementary glimpses into the same life and love of the Creator God.

The third and final example of a single covenant theologian that we shall examine is A. Roy Eckardt, although here too he may not fit the label precisely anymore in view of some recent changes in his outlook. Over the years Eckardt has consistently maintained that Christianity has not taken Israel's place in salvation history and that Israel's divine vocation remains intact into our day. God's faithfulness to Israel means that the covenant continues unbroken. It is this covenant that requires Israel to reject Jesus as the Messiah. He holds that God's purpose was that a majority of Israel should not accept Jesus. Eckardt concludes that Israel and the church stand in dialectical tension to each other within the one covenant. Each has a different function and a corresponding temptation. Israel's primary role is to face inward to the Jewish people while Christianity's function is to look outward toward the Gentiles. The corresponding temptations are that the Jew may let his or her election lead to self-exaltation and the Christian's reliance on grace may lead to absolution from all duties under the law. Or, in opposing a false dichotomizing between the sacred and the profane, Israel may secularize the Kingdom of God; on the other hand, in going forth into the secular world Christianity may be tempted to over-spiritualize the Kingdom of God and negate the goodness of creation. As Eckardt sees it,

> Jesus of Nazareth, called the Christ, embodies the paradox of uniting Jews with Christians and of separating Jews from Christians. There is simply no way around or beyond this stern fact. Any discussion of the Jewish-Christian relationship must presuppose both elements in this ultimate tension. The mystery of Israel's election has found a continuation and fulfillment in the mystery of the incarnation of God in Jesus Christ.[45]

For Eckardt the revelation in Jesus Christ, though unique in some respects, is in principle no greater than the revelation brought forth through the divine actions whereby Israel gained her election. A Christian theology of Judaism is called to proclaim, according to Eckardt, that the church stands as successor to Israel only in one respect. In virtue of the ministry of Jesus the wall that had divided Jews and Gentiles has been permanently destroyed. The abiding covenant with the people Israel has been opened to the nations of the world in a manner that Judaism never quite envisioned.

In some recent writings, Eckardt has begun to hedge somewhat about his single covenant orientation. He feels that perhaps the Christian community must enable Israel to move in whatever direction she sees fit, even if this means severing covenantal ties. He has maintained a single covenant stance for many years because of his great concern about Christian supersessionist approaches to Judaism. But once Christianity has overcome the perverse desire to replace "old Israel," it may be perfectly legitimate for the two faith communities in love and respect to go their separate ways.[46]

As Eckardt has developed his thought further, especially in light of his research on the Nazi holocaust, he seems to be moving in the direction of saying that many of the theological categories we have traditionally used to describe the Jewish-Christian encounter are no longer valid. Both Judaism and Christianity must be re-thought in the light of the shattering experience that the holocaust represents. In studies prepared for an ongoing group of Christian theologians called the Israel Study Group, Eckardt has suggested among other things that perhaps we can no longer speak of the Jews as a covenanted people in traditional terms and that the Christian doctrine of the resurrection must be dropped from the credo if we are ever to correct finally the classical Christian distortion of Judaism. Auschwitz has for him undercut the traditional belief in God's faithfulness to Israel. The old understanding of the covenant was "consumed once and for all in the flames of the crematoria, its breath was snuffed out forever in the gas chambers."[47] There only remains room for a covenant of the divine agony which places the Jewish people in a state of unqualified ordinariness, of absolute secularity within this world.

Auschwitz also means the end of any continuing belief in Jesus' resurrection. It is not as much a question of the Nazi holocaust wiping out this traditional Christian claim for Eckardt as it is that Auschwitz finally and decisively showed the error of that belief in the first place. For Christians today who are serious about ending the church's degradation of Judaism resurrection can have only a future connotation. Eckardt writes:

> That Jewish man from the Galilee sleeps now. He sleeps with the other Jewish dead, with all the disconsolate and scattered ones of the murder camps, and with the unnumbered dead of the human and non-human family. But Jesus of Nazareth shall be raised. So too shall the small Hungarian children who were burned alive at Auschwitz.[48]

Eckardt goes on to say that Jesus' coming resurrection will have special meaning for Christians because it is his history through which the Gentiles were brought into the covenant with Israel. In the same way, the future resurrection of Abraham and Moses will carry distinctive significance for the eschatological community of Jews. This presentation would seem to place Eckardt back into the single school of thought even though he has drastically re-interpreted the understanding of the covenantal tradition. It is not clear where he stands at the moment regarding the reservations about a single covenant which he expressed in 1974. Without doubt his thinking on the matter remains fluid.

Moving on now to the double covenant school we shall first look at the perspective of J. Coert Rylaarsdam. After long experience in the dialogue, Rylaarsdam has concluded that the basic tension between Judaism and Christianity can only be understood by recognizing the existence of two distinctive covenants within the thought world of biblical Judaism. The first, the covenant with Israel, represents the side of history and signifies a socio-religious union called into being by God. It includes a mutual pact of faithfulness and responsibility between God and his people. This covenant is characterized by the continuity between gospel and law and includes both the motif of the recital of the covenant and the motif of obligation. The biblical themes of the first covenant reflect the belief that the only significant world is that of people and history, especially as seen through the particularity of Israel which has been chosen by Yahweh. This covenant is future directed. The events it relates constitute a salvation history replete with "acts of divine rescue." It remains an open history. This salvation history cannot easily be blended with the Christ Event. Hence it was not as significant for the New Testament writers as the second covenant.

The second covenant is the covenant with David. As

interpreted by Rylaarsdam, it represents the eschatological tradition. The principal characteristic of this covenant
is the holiness attached to Mt. Zion and the divine presence as revealed through the dynasty of David. The appearance of this covenantal tradition marked a new beginning. It continued to stand in tension with the first
covenant to which it was finally accommodated though
without total absorption. This covenant alludes to and
celebrates a supratemporal order of significance. God is
king of creation and of the nations. "Law" and "history"
are largely absent from its area of concern. Whereas one
finds no Alpha-Omega aspect in the future-oriented first
covenant, the second celebrates Alpha with emphasis on
its meaning for the present.

Rylaarsdam believes that the ongoing tension between these two covenants ultimately produced several
sects, one of which became the eschatologically oriented
Christian church. The new faith tradition contained the
same tension as biblical Judaism but with a reversal in
the priority of the two covenants. In the words of Rylaarsdam:

> However Jesus may have understood his voca-
> tion, at the outset Christians interpreted his ca-
> reer as an eschatological event. He had over-
> come the world (*olam*), relativized history—or
> even abolished it. Except for some sectarian
> movements, Judaism thought more historically
> than eschatologically; it awaited the transfor-
> mation and redemption of the world. So the
> Jews said that the Messiah had not come. But
> the Gentiles believed. And the Christians wrote
> a commentary on the Hebrew Bible and called
> it the New Testament. Its accent is overwhelm-

ingly eschatological. Therefore it has now become the primary occasion for the dilemmas of
Christology.[49]

Rylaarsdam emphasizes that the Christians who auth-
ored the New Testament were a Jewish sect. They were
sectarian because they took such a one-sided view of the
relation of the two covenants to one another. For a moment they forgot about the paradoxical character of the
relationship, and they thought that the full meaning of
human history could be fitted into the perspective of the
eschatological. Yet soon they appear to have seen the error of their ways. Nineteen centuries of Christian history
can be viewed, according to Rylaarsdam, as the story of a
progressive attempt to overcome this initial mistake. In
this task the fact that the church retained the Hebrew
Scriptures as part of its Bible has proved most useful
since it has kept some link between Christianity and its
Jewish roots.

There are then for Rylaarsdam two covenants in the
Christian Bible. They are not the two covenants usually
called old and new testaments, placed *seriatim*. Rather
the two covenants run through both the Hebrew Scriptures and the New Testament. In view of this the relationship between the two faiths emerges as something
radically other than the traditional Christian statement of
it. If both Judaism and Christianity always continue to
revolve around the same two covenants that are para-
doxically related to one another, then their relationship,
whatever its actual tension, is forever mutually interdependent.

The pioneering scholar in twentieth-century Christian-Jewish dialogue James Parkes anchors his version of
the "double-covenant" theory in what he calls the differ-

ent but complementary revelations of "Sinai" and "Calvary." Sinai centers around the community while Calvary focuses on the understanding of the individual person:

> That highest purpose of God which Sinai reveals to men as community, Calvary reveals to man as an end in himself. The difference between the two events, both of which from the metaphysical standpoint are identical as expressions of the infinite in the finite, of the eternal in the world of space and time, lies in the fact that the first could not be fulfilled by a brief demonstration of a divine community in action; but the second could not be fulfilled except by a life lived under human conditions from birth to death.[50]

Parkes claims that a stress on the person as individual began to grow in Jewish literature in the exilic and post-exilic periods. Witness, he says, the concern with the individual in Jeremiah, Ezekiel, the Wisdom literature, Job and among the Pharisees. It is out of this movement that Jesus stepped into history. The revelation of Calvary did not replace Sinai, nor could Sinai simply absorb it and remain unchanged. In the life and teaching of Jesus the earlier revelation and the new revelation co-exist in creative tension. In the Christian concern with the individual as person, nothing is taken away from the power or import of the working out in history of the revelation of Sinai. Sinai did not mark the beginning of human concern with the moral problems of people in society. Behind Sinai were centuries of experience which were both human discoveries and divine revelations. What occurred at Sinai was the full development of a long gradual growth in the human person's understanding of community. It took centuries to realize the full extent of Sinai and even today it remains difficult to define the complete meaning of that revelation. In the same manner what had been growing in Judaism since the period of the exile attained its full development with Calvary and has been subject to interpretation ever since:

> The divine plan for human society is given its full meaning when the divine plan for man as person is revealed within it. In Jesus the ultimate unity is not destroyed; Paul still struggles to maintain it. But in the complex setting of first-century life the two halves broke apart, and the beginning of the second century witnessed two religions confronting each other—Judaism and Christianity.[51]

For Parkes, Judaism and Christianity are inextricably linked together as equals. The tension that exists between them is not rooted in some metaphysic forced upon history from without, but in the perennial and inevitable experience of tension in ordinary human life between the human person as social being and as individual, as an ultimate value in himself or herself, as one formed in the likeness of God. This tension extends to the whole of life and will endure so long as the world endures.

A third representative of the double-covenant school is Rosemary Ruether. As we have already seen, she feels deeply that any ultimate resolution of the centuries of Christian disdain for Jews and Judaism can come about only with the development of a renewed Christology. The roots of the long-standing tradition of Christian anti-Semitism are to be found in the Christologies developed within the New Testament and "perfected" by the Church Fathers.

Ruether takes the position that the Messianic Age did not come to pass in the Christ Event, something she believes emerges as an inescapable fact of history, something with which Christians have not sufficiently reckoned up till now. In her eyes human history remains as much, perhaps even more mired in ambiguity, sickness, sin and death as it was prior to the coming of Jesus. If the church wants to affirm that the term "Christ" refers to the Messiah of Israel's hope, then it must also come to appreciate that "from the standpoint of that faith of Israel itself, there is no possibility of talking about the Messiah having come (much less of having come two thousand years ago, with all the evil history that has reigned from that time until this), when the reign of God has not come."[52] She bluntly affirms that "what Christianity has in Jesus is not the Messiah, but a Jew who hoped for the Kingdom of God and who died in that hope."[53]

For the Jewish tradition, in Ruether's view, the coming of the Messiah and the appearance of the Messianic Age are simultaneous. They are in actuality the same event. In Judaism the stress has always been placed primarily on the Messianic Age rather than on the person of the Messiah. The difficulty is that Christianity took this traditional Jewish belief in the Messianic Age of the future and "imported" it into present history. It declared evil to have been conquered once and for all by the Christ Event. As a result, the ultimate crisis of human existence, the crisis that divides the historical from the eschatological, was falsely solved. All human history before Christ could be viewed as the period of unredeemed humanity. All those who fail to accept the Christian revelation, especially Jews, continue to live in this era. Through Christian faith, however, men and women can pass into the new historical period of messianic glory. Instead of an aid for illuminating the tension between the historical and the eschatological, Christian messianism has become the instrument for developing a false consciousness, "allowing the church to dress historical ambiguities in the dress of finality and absolute truth. This new historical era and people are seen as standing, not merely in a relative but in an absolute super-sessionary relationship to Judaism and to all human possibilities 'before Christ'."[54] Ruether calls this process the illegitimate historicizing of the eschatological.

Messianism in Christianity cannot have any validity for Ruether unless it points to an ultimate, future coming of the Messiah which will mark the end of suffering and injustice on this earth. The attribution of an absolute finality to the expectations that arose because of the ministry and death of Jesus represents a flawed way of appropriating the authentic meaning of eschatology. Very serious consequences have resulted from this historicizing of the eschatology. Both Christian anti-Semitism and the patterns of totalitarianism and imperialism that have manifested themselves in Christian history find their justification in this false assumption

The traditional idea that the final Messianic event has already occurred in Jesus needs to be reformulated. Ruether does not offer any comprehensive reformulation. This remains a serious deficiency in her overall approach to the question. She does indicate in a general way that such a reformulation must begin by taking seriously the insights of the theology of hope. The messianic meaning of Jesus' ministry under such a perspective would assume a paradigmatic and anticipatory function; it did not bring about a final completion of human history. But this understanding of the meaning of the eschatological experience in Jesus also demands a certain relativizing of it with respect to other faith communities who have not shared in this paradigmatic experience. The cross and the resurrection are eschatological paradigms only for those who have consciously accepted them as such. Those people who have not accepted these paradigms because they have others which emerge from their own histories as more compelling should not be regarded as unredeemed nor should their faith perspective be branded as false. "This contextual view of the significance of the cross and the resurrection," says Ruether, "takes seriously the diversity of peoples and their histories, out of which they hear God through the memory of different revelatory experiences."[55]

A final example of those who would regard the Jewish-Christian relationship as essentially discontinuous is the biblical scholar E.P. Sanders. In a recent study which has all the qualifications to become a classic work entitled *Paul and Palestinian Judaism*[56] Sanders has thoroughly researched Palestinian Judaism in the Second Temple period and how it relates to major theological themes in the Pauline corpus. No recent Christian scholar has exhibited as thorough an understanding of Second Temple Judaism as Sanders. His study has led him to two principal conclusions: there was a generally prevalent religious outlook in Palestinian Judaism which can be called "covenantal nomism"; the Pauline pattern of religious thought was basically different, emphasizing "participationist eschatology." Thus Sanders would say that Christianity, at least to the considerable extent that Paul formulated its basic theological stance, is a different type of religion than Judaism. While he does not delve into the theological implications of this conclusion in any comprehensive fashion, he does state quite clearly his belief that there is no inherent reason for thinking one superior to the other. In fact, Sanders observes that the Pauline position could not be maintained consistently in the church in any pure sense.

> Christianity rapidly became a new covenantal nomism, but Paulinism is not thereby proved inferior or superior. In saying that participationist eschatology is different from covenantal nomism, I mean only to say that it is different, not that the difference is instructive for seeing the error of Judaism's way.[57]

Hence, without being entirely clear on the matter, Sanders would seem to grant equal status to both Judaism and Christianity, thereby undercutting much of traditional Christian theology regarding Judaism. There are also obvious implications in this for the ultimate significance of the Christ Event, but Sanders chooses not to elaborate on this. Rather than presenting any reformulation of Christology, Sanders' research provides a new base for such reformulation that no serious theologian can ignore.

Having examined some representative viewpoints among Christian scholars who have devoted special attention to the Jewish-Christian relationship, we can now look at how a select number of major figures in contemporary theology handle the question. Two recent general works on the subject by Eva Fleischner[58] and Charlotte Klein[59] clearly show that overall contemporary Christian theology has not treated this relationship with much enlightenment. In her study of major German theological literature since World War II, Dr. Fleischner finds that many important figures such as Johannes Metz, Walter Kasper and Karl Rahner have almost totally ignored the question of Judaism. Dr. Klein, in her survey of biblical and theological materials, has uncovered a pervasive anti-Judaism, especially among scholars in continental Europe. She attributes this prejudice to an almost total lack of acquaintance on the part of these scholars with serious Jewish research on the Second Temple period in Judaism. They have tended to rely exclusively on outdated Christian research on the subject. The picture in the Anglo-American world she found somewhat more encouraging. Scholars working in this milieu seem to have a greater familiarity with the pioneering study of Judaism done by Christian scholars such as R. Travers Herford and George F. Moore and with the range of contemporary Jewish opinion on the developments in the period.

Turning now to a few specific viewpoints, we first encounter the thought of Wolfhart Pannenberg. In his major volume, *Jesus, God and Man* he asserts that with the resurrection of Christ the foundations of the Jewish religion collapsed. No attempt at improving relations with Jews can ever obscure this fact for Pannenberg. The rejection of the Jewish law by Jesus was the basis for his conflict with the Jewish authorities. We cannot lose sight of this. As Pannenberg bluntly puts it, " . . . either Jesus had been a blasphemer or the law of the Jews—and with it Judaism itself as a religion—is done away with."[60]

In a subsequent volume, which followed Pannenberg's first visit to the United States, he indicates some modification of his viewpoint on Judaism. Saying that he deeply regrets the rigidity of the perspective he offered on Jesus and Second Temple Judaism in his earlier volume, Pannenberg indicates he is now prepared to accept a distinction between the "religion of the law" condemned by

Jesus and Judaism as such. He confesses that he was a victim of the widespread attitude in German Protestantism that the religion of the law and the Jewish religion are identical. The God of Jewish history can stand above the Law—this he is now able to acknowledge. For it is only in this way that the ministry of Jesus can be understood as a Jewish phenomenon. Pannenberg recognizes that this shift of viewpoint makes possible greater open-mindedness toward dialogue between Christians and Jews since it takes account of the broad common basis which links Christianity and Judaism despite their profound contrasts.[61]

The difficulty with Pannenberg's corrective statements in his 1972 volume is that they are found in a relatively unimportant work in comparison to *Jesus, God and Man* which has received widespread attention. Many Christians still assume that Pannenberg stands by the earlier version of his theology of Judaism. This became clear in 1974 when the American Theological Society discussed this topic and it became painfully evident that few, if any, participants were aware of what he had written subsequently on the matter. In an afterword which Pannenberg has prepared for a second edition of *Jesus, God and Man* he calls the reader's attention in a footnote to his shift in position on the Jewish question, citing the pertinent passages from his 1972 volume. But the body of the text in the second edition has remained unchanged. So this important work in contemporary theological reformulation retains the potential for leaving its readership with an unbalanced understanding of Judaism in the time of Jesus.

Another outstanding figure on the contemporary Protestant theological scene is Professor Jurgen Moltmann. In his work of theological construction he has claimed that the shattering events associated with the Nazi holocaust profoundly condition the interpretations he now offers of the Christian gospel. In a major volume called *The Crucified God* he devotes considerable attention to the question of Judaism. His general attitudes show a great similarity to the traditional approach to gospel and law dominant in German Protestantism. We find his interpretation of the trial of Jesus largely centering on Jesus' rejection of the Jewish legal tradition. In this he comes close to Pannenberg's outlook in *Jesus, God and Man*. The core of Moltmann's exegesis in this regard can be seen in the following passage:

> (Jesus') execution must be seen as a necessary consequence of his conflict with the law. His trial by the guardians of the law was in the broader sense of the term a trial about the will of God, which the law claimed to have codified once for all. Here the conflict between Jesus and the law was not a dispute about a different will, or the will of a different God, but about the true will of God, which for Jesus was hidden and not revealed by the human concept of the law.[62]

Moltmann goes on to say that the conflict between law and gospel in the teaching of Jesus must be related to the promise of Abraham. He argues that through the gospel this promise of life was liberated from the shadow of a legalist understanding of the law and given universal force for everyone who believes, be he or she Jew or Gentile. Moltmann insists that only the crucified God can bring the freedom which changes the world because the fear of death has vanished. The church of the crucified God can liberate all men and women, including Jews. Moltmann does recognize that the continuing existence of Israel shows the church that the redemption of the world is still to come. Christians share an inescapable solidarity with the people Israel, "not only with the Israel of the Old Testament, but also with the Israel which rightfully exists alongside the church and which in consequence cannot be abolished."[63] For Moltmann the church remains incomplete and the Kingdom of God has not yet attained the fullness of revelation so long as the two communities of hope live side by side. He warns that no Christian can accept the position that Israel is the old "religion of the law" which since the death and resurrection of Christ has been pushed to the side by the Christian "religion of love."

Moltmann thus shows a sensitivity to Judaism and to the historic Jewish-Christian relationship that is absent from the writings of most of his theological colleagues. Yet, the question that A. Roy Eckardt asks Moltmann in his critique of *The Crucified God* remains valid: what is the possible ground for asserting that Israel exists by right and should not be abolished?[64] In short, in this work, Moltmann has not yet adequately developed a comprehensive theology of Judaism that really establishes the validity of its ongoing, independent existence as a faith community.

Moltmann's latest volume *The Church in the Power of the Spirit: A Contribution to Messianic Ecclesiology* shows some significant advances in his thinking about the role of Judaism. Especially important are a new emphasis on the unique solidarity Christians ought to have with Israel, the conviction that the relationship with Israel takes priority for Christianity over all other external relations, and the belief that Judaism is the foundation for the

church both past and future. Without hesitation Moltmann argues that the church's history of anti-Judaism
has been directly responsible for its paganization. He
calls for an end to Christian triumphalism with respect to
Judaism which in the concrete implies a rediscovery of
the relevance of the Hebrew Scriptures, a new appreciation of the unfulfilled nature of messianic hope, and the
placing of Israel in a position of partnership with the
church. Israel retains her sacred mission alongside Christianity until the end of days. Of special note is Moltmann's contention that Christian hatred of the so-called
"obdurate Jew" constitutes in reality an exercise in
Christian self-hatred. He displays a much deeper understanding and appreciation of the Jewish Torah tradition
than in *The Crucified God.* He also condemns all Christian super-sessionist doctrines about Judaism and feels
that the re-establishment of the modern State of Israel
has placed the Christian-Jewish relations on an entirely
new level.

Yet some serious flaws remain in the latest version
of Moltmann's theology of Judaism. He supports the position that with the second coming of Christ Christian
hope and Jewish hope alike will be brought to completion. At the parousia Christ will reveal himself as the
Messiah of Israel. Through their rejection of Christ Jews
will be the last to enter the kingdom. Again the critique
of A. Roy Eckardt has merit with respect to Moltmann's
latest stance. Eckardt argues that in *The Church in the
Power of the Spirit* anti-Judaism has merely been tem-
pered, not finally overcome: " . . . the church *does* constitute the practical replacement of Israel in the work of salvation. The church remains, in Moltmann's view, the
(round-about) instrument of the salvation of Israel."[66]

Turning to the Catholic scene, we find at least two

prominent systematicians beginning to take the existence of Judaism much more seriously in their theological construction. Hans Kung has been in many ways the one to break new ground in this regard. In his widely read volume *On Being a Christian*[67] Kung states in the strongest possible terms that after the Nazi holocaust Christians cannot avoid a clear admission of guilt for the centuries of anti-Judaism within the church. Together with the re-emergence of the State of Israel (which Kung calls "the most important event in Jewish history since the destruction of Jerusalem and the Temple") it has undercut the pseudo-theology of Judaism propagated by Christians for centuries. No longer can the church claim that the Jews are cursed as a people because of their rejection of Jesus or overlook their permanent election which was asserted by St. Paul on the excuse that this election has now been transferred to Christians as the new Israel. Too often the church has stood between Israel and Jesus. For Kung, the present task of the church is not to try to convert Jews, but to be converted itself to a humanitarian and theological encounter with Jews that might provide its members with new self-understanding.

Kung does not really elaborate in *On Being a Christian* what a reformulated Christian theology of Judaism would look like. He does say, however, that perhaps Jews could help Christians conduct a new search for the meaning of Jesus *from below* and that Jews too need to rethink the religious significance of Jesus from within the Jewish tradition.

In a 1975 radio dialogue in Germany with the Orthodox Jewish scholar Pinchas Lapide which has been published in the *"Journal of Ecumenical Studies"*[68] and most recently in Kung's new volume *Signposts for the Future*[69] he addresses the question what it is that on the whole distinguishes Christianity from Judaism. He says somewhat tersely that it remains the reality that has separated the two communities from the outset: Jesus as the Christ is rejected by the Jews and accepted by the Christian community. The precise title under which the church recognizes Christ is not all-important. The various titles, Son of God, Son of Man, Lord, etc., are not decisive in their own right. What is crucial is acceptance of Jesus as the authoritative standard. He remains for Christian believers not merely one among many archetypal human beings, but the archetype above all others. This is the real difference in Kung's mind, since in Jewish eyes the law is the authoritative standard and not Jesus of Nazareth.

In keeping with the orientation expressed in *On Being a Christian* Kung stresses in this radio dialogue that the issue for Christians is not simply developing a doctrine about Christ, but of following his example. He is convinced that the whole history of the relations between Christians and Jews would have taken a different turn if Christians as practical disciples of Christ had tried to incorporate his loving attitudes toward the Jews and their religious tradition instead of merely disputing with Jews on a theoretical level how the Christ Event is to be explained. While such an emphasis has merit, it really skirts the major issue. Action will always be based, consciously or unconsciously, on some theory. Kung, though exhibiting great sensitivity for the past and present situation of the Jewish people, still needs to go much further in rethinking the Christian theology of Judaism. He still has not offered any sound reasons why Christians should look upon Judaism as a valid religious tradition after Christ and what Christians might learn from Judaism and vice versa.

The Dutch Catholic theologian Edward Schille-beeckx has come to the discussion of Judaism well after Hans Kung. But his approach is somewhat more comprehensive. In the first part of his recently published volume *Christology*[70] (not yet available in English), he takes up several major questions relating to the Jewish-Christian encounter. He examines first of all Jesus' attitude toward the Torah. He rejects any notion that Jesus intended to abrogate the Law in virtue of his divine authority. Following in the tradition of the prophets Jesus radicalized the Law, as Schillebeeckx sees the situation. This radicalization, however, also implied a certain relativization of those specific laws which tended to block a return to the authentic relationship to Torah which enhances people's humanity and liberates God from oppressive imagery. Those passages in the New Testament which depict Jesus as challenging the Torah from his position as the Christ were not part of Jesus' own attitude. Rather than transcending the Law, the Jesus of Schillebeeckx's theology emerges almost as a rigorist in the tradition of the Jewish apocalyptic sects, demanding a return to the full spirit and letter of God's Torah.

The repentance and conversion Jesus urged upon his Jewish brothers and sisters would prepare them for the coming of the reign of God in Israel. Only if Israel truly followed the Torah could God's Reign be established. Jesus is seen by Schillebeeckx as the authentic teacher of the Law who exposes the deepest salvific intentions of the Torah: freeing the human person for good. Schillebeeckx sees this as entirely consistent with current Jewish interpretations of the Law. Together with the experience of God as Father, this thrust constitutes the essence of Jesus' preaching.

After the death of Jesus, the church began the pro-

cess of interpreting the meaning of his ministry for future
generations. Schillebeeckx is of the opinion that he was
eventually identified with the prophet of the endtime,
filled with and anointed by God's Spirit, who would
bring the Good News of salvation, namely that God
would reign. This identification, however, did not involve
simply choosing one among the models that were then
present within the existing currents of Judaism. Various
models had an influence: the anointed of God, the Messiah, the Son of Man. The Son of David model also had a
part, especially the prophetic-sapiential strain that combined a nonpolitical Son of David with the concept of
messenger found in II Isaiah. Thus the confession of Jesus as the Christ was the result of the mixture of several
messianic models from the Judaism of the period. In no
way did it constitute the creation of a new messianic vision in total opposition to Judaism. It represented a conscious selection of various ideas from within Jewish messianic thinking of the first century.

Over and over again in this volume Schillebeeckx affirms that the earliest Christology in the church was a totally Jewish phenomenon, and that the basic formative
period of Christology worked within the framework of
the Judaism of the day. The break with Judaism, the ex-
pulsion from the Synagogue, was the work of certain
dominant elements within Palestinian Judaism. On the
other hand, Jesus remained attractive to significant num-
bers of Hellenistic Jews.

In an exploration of the potential of Schillebeeckx's
recent thought for improving Christian-Jewish understanding, Professor Robert Schreiter of the Catholic
Theological Union has highlighted the following elements.[71] Schillebeeckx portrays the original conflict between church and synagogue as one stemming more from

the inherent sociology of sectarian movements rather
than clear-cut doctrinal disagreements. It was not a question of Christianity rebelling against a monolithic Jewish
orthodoxy. The church developed its interpretations of
Jesus largely within the parameters of Second Temple Judaism. But the destruction of the Temple at Jerusalem
and the attempt by rabbinic leadership to impose some
unity within Palestinian Judaism in the hope of surviving
the destruction intensified differences already existing
within Judaism. Christianity, far from united internally,
found itself in conflict with an emerging Jewish orthodoxy as did some of the other movements within Second
Temple Judaism. The polemics of Paul, the passionate
convert, were a prelude to what would become a sectarian pattern in the canonical literature of the New Testament: Christianity struggling to establish its distinctive
identity apart from other Jewish groups by claiming for
itself the only authentic interpretation of the Hebrew
Scriptures.

Thus in the perspective offered by Schillebeeckx,
Christianity in its origins reflects the tensions within the
Jewish community in which the church was born. In its
polemic against other Jewish movements of the time
Christianity may have buried important aspects of its
original religious heritage. The need to appear different
and superior, common to most sectarian movements,
may account at least partially for the increasing shift toward a triumphal ecclesiology and a shift away from Jewish models for speaking about the relationship between
Jesus and God in favor of Greek ones, a process that
reached culmination at the Council of Chalcedon. These
models would become the touchstone for much of the future anti-Semitism in the church. Schreiter makes it clear
that in the theology of Schillebeeckx the sharpness of the

polemic against the Jews only makes sense in view of "the shared roots of two estranged brothers."[72]

To deal with Schillebeeckx's understanding of the root cause of traditional Christian-Jewish hostility, Schreiter makes several concrete suggestions in line with Schillebeeckx's overall theological stance. First of all, by concentrating on the sociological aspects of first-century church-synagogue relations rather than the doctrinal dimensions we might be able to see the surface level polemics of the writings involved as rather unsuccessful attempts to mediate the human tensions involved in such contraries as the Torah of the heart versus the Torah of ritual or following tradition meticulously over against a desire to go beyond it. Secondly, Schillebeeckx's suggestions that we must take statements about Christian fulfillment as anticipatory instead of participatory with regard to the Reign of God allows room for a fresh discussion of such key Christian concepts as Messiah, salvation and eschatology. Finally, if we understand the anti-Judaic strain in Christology as stemming in part at least from the church's inability to face up to the historical failure of Jesus' preaching of the Reign of God (which Schillebeeckx views as one of the poles of Jesus' ministry), we might be in a position to turn around such anti-Judaism by approaching such "failure-in-meaning" in a new way. Rather than simply try to cover-up such failure, in this case projecting the fulfillment of God's Reign to a nonhistorical sphere, we might come to appreciate that such failure clears the ground for the emergence of other faith meanings. Using this interpretative tool with respect to anti-Judaic texts will open the door for the creation of a new theology of Judaism.

It is encouraging to find such a major figure in contemporary theology sensitive to the historic tensions between Judaism and Christianity. His stress on these tensions as more sociological than doctrinal is a welcome contribution to the discussion of the question. The same may be said for the theological method he suggests for handling the polemical texts. He lays firm ground for the possibility of building a new theology of Judaism in the church that need not be totally bound by the surface meaning of the classical texts. This, in itself, represents a major breakthrough in theological methodology.

But, like Kung, Schillebeeckx avoids some of the central issues about the meaning of the Christ Event vis-à-vis the continuing validity of Judaism. Does Christianity possess an essential content of salvation which Judaism lacks? Is Christ meant ultimately as the Savior of the Jews as Moltmann implies? In this regard Schillebeeckx, who seems to share with Moltmann a belief in the anticipatory nature of the proclamation about the presence of God's Reign, is much more vague than Moltmann in spelling out the ultimate implications of this position. Because of his lack of candidness in this regard, it is difficult to know whether Eckardt's criticisms of Moltmann could be applied with equal force to Schillebeeckx as well. Perhaps Schillebeeckx's second volume on Christology will make his position clearer in this area.

This brief examination of how Christian scholars have treated the question of Judaism in the light of Christology certainly elucidates the lack of consensus in the matter. There is no clear agreement even among the exegetes and theologians who have devoted considerable research time to Jewish-Christian questions. And the thought of the major systematicians who have only begun to grapple seriously with Judaism obviously bears the marks of infancy. Against a background of considerable diversity, and that is putting it mildly, can we draw together any conclusions about the status of the contemporary Christian re-examination of Judaism? Some directions do seem to be emerging, and the following would be chief among them.

(1) We are coming to the end of the time when it will be acceptable for any serious Christian scholar to claim that Jesus was the expected Jewish Messiah or that the Reign of God in human history was fulfilled by his coming. Nor will it be possible any longer for Christians to contrast the difference between Judaism and Christianity by law-grace, law-love, or law-freedom with the implied superiority of the Christian way of life in each case. There is a growing consensus that the whole theology of Judaism will have to be reformulated by Christian theologians. And this reformulation will necessitate some adjustment in traditional Christological interpretation.

(2) In the process of building anew the church's theological outlook on Judaism there will be need to take more seriously the research on developments within Second Temple Judaism and on the sociological aspects of the animosity that developed between church and synagogue in the first century. In particular, the discoveries of contemporary Jewish scholarship on the Second Temple period will have to play a much more significant role than in the past where they were practically ignored. Schillebeeckx and Sanders have provided some worthwhile initial models in this regard. The major systematicians will also need to become better acquainted with the thought of those theologians and biblical scholars who have specialized in the Christian-Jewish dialogue. Thus far the contact has been minimal.

(3) In developing a reformulated theology of Judaism it is difficult at this point to say whether terms like "double covenant," "single covenant," "continuity/discontin-

uity" are helpful anymore in describing the relationship between church and synagogue. It may be that new terms will have to be found. On the one hand, it is imperative to maintain the close link historically between Judaism and Christianity. The Judaic base of early Christianity needs to be recovered in our time not only for the sake of better relations between Christians and Jews, but for authentic Christian self-renewal as well. On the other hand, it is equally important to recognize that since the time of separation Judaism and Christianity have become two distinct religious traditions. Each has developed a fundamentally different religious ethos in the course of centuries of separate development. Hence it serves no purpose, in fact it has the contrary effect, for Christians to refer glibly to the so-called "Judaeo-Christian" tradition. While use of this term is generally well-intentioned, the criticism of Jewish scholars such as Arthur Cohen[73] and Hans Jonas[74] that reference to a single Judaeo-Christian tradition represents a basic distortion of reality in which the uniqueness of Judaism is obscured is fundamentally on target.

Any new theology of Judaism within Christianity will have to begin with the insight offered by E.P. Sanders. In summarizing his research on Pauline theology and Judaism he says that there are "substantial agreements and a basic difference. Further, the difference is not located in a supposed antithesis of grace and works (on grace and works there is in fact agreement, and an agreement which can hardly be called 'peripheral'), but in the total type of religion."[75] This new theology of Judaism will also have to grapple with distinctions offered by scholars such as James Parkes and J. Coert Rylaarsdam. It will need to take seriously Rosemary Ruether's insistence that Christianity suffered serious distortion by projecting the Jewish sense of the Kingdom of God arriving within history to a non-historical, spiritual dimension.

But in reanchoring Christian eschatology in history it will also be necessary to understand that in the process of what Ruether calls "the spiritualizing of the eschatological" the very basis for developing an authentic theology of Christianity that does not automatically invalidate the Jewish covenant may be found. It is at this point that Ruether's reflections show a serious weakness. While pointing out the unfortunate directions that this process took, she fails to appreciate how it was part of the development within Second Temple Judaism that was looking for a deeper relationship between history and human consciousness than the earlier Exodus covenant tradition had provided.[76] The later Paul and the gospel of John picked up on this trend in their Christological developments. It is this reality which Schillebeeckx highlights when he stresses that for Jesus the experience of God as Abba was crucial and which Sanders correctly perceives in his analysis of Pauline theology as fundamentally rooted in participation in Christ. Finally, this trend will lead to what emerges as *the* difference between Christianity and Judaism as religions—not the notion of Jesus as the expected Jewish Messiah, but the notion of the Incarnation. In constructing their theological views of Judaism, Van Buren, Ruether and Kung have not dealt adequately with this difference.

While undertaking the task of creating a new theology of Judaism Christian theologians will also have to search for a way to define the uniqueness of Christianity. This is not simply a call to pick up the attempts earlier on in this century to find the "essence of Christianity." Most of these stripped Christianity of its inherent Jewish base. But more depth and uniqueness will have to be found within the Christian religious tradition than merely calling it "Judaism for the Gentiles" for it to survive as a separate religion. We need to arrive at a point where we see both Judaism and Christianity as religious traditions which share something of a common biblical heritage, but are essentially distinct religions, each with its own self-integrity, each emphasizing different but ultimately complementary aspects of human religiosity.

(4) Concomitant with the search for the uniqueness of Christianity vis-à-vis Judaism must be the clear admission on the part of Christian theologians that Christianity in and by itself does not contain in their fullness all the insights or experiences necessary for a complete understanding of the religious dimension of the human person and that only through interfaith sharing can we even begin to approach such an understanding. Such admission is demanded now even though it is not yet possible to articulate in any complete fashion a new definition of Christianity's role vis-à-vis Judaism than other world religions. Humble acknowledgment by the church that its previous viewpoint was shortsighted is the imperative of the time. There will also be need for Christian theologians to probe non-Christian religions more deeply to see whether it might not be possible that the fundamental reality to which Christianity has applied the term "Christ" may not in fact be present under some other name or symbol.

(5) An issue that directly flows from the discussion of a new theology of Judaism within the church is that of Christian missionizing of the Jewish people. This has been an intensely discussed matter both within Judaism and within certain sectors of Protestant Christianity in particular. In an article entitled "Christian Missionaries and a Jewish Response"[77] Rabbi Balfour Brickner, long a

participant in the interreligious dialogue on behalf of the
Union of American Hebrew Congregations, takes Protestant denominations to task for not seriously confronting
the issue of proselytizing Jews who see the matter as one
of community survival. He feels the Catholic community
has done somewhat better in this regard, especially with
the presentation made in March 1977 by Professor Tomasso Federici of the Pontifical University Propaganda
Fide in Rome to the International Catholic-Jewish Liai-
son Committee sponsored by the Vatican and international Jewish organizations. In this paper Professor Federici clearly repudiates any missionizing goal for the
Catholic Church regarding Jews. If the Catholic Church
understood its mission in this way at one time, it was a
mistake due to an inaccurate understanding of the irrevo-
cability of God's promise to the Jewish people and of the
enternality of his covenant with them.[78]

The issue is far from settled in any of the branches of
the Christian church. Several Protestant clergyman took
strong exception to Rabbi Brickner in letters to *"Worldview."*[79] Professor Gerald H. Anderson, long involved in
Christian missionary efforts, insists that biblical faithfulness demands that Jews be included, even with priority,
in the general mandate given by Christ to evangelize all
the nations. And the *"National Catholic Register"* severe-
ly criticized the paper by Dr. Federici in its edition of
July 10, 1977, claiming that if the Christians do not believe Jews should become Christians, there is no reason
for them to stay Christian themselves. There is no solution to the dilemma about Christian attempts to evangelize Jews apart from a total re-examination of the
church's Christological traditions and their relationship
to the theology of Judaism. The changed Christian attitude toward the ongoing authenticity of the Jewish cov-

enant, based on a new understanding of the Christ Event, will of necessity demand rethinking of the meaning of mission in relationship to the people Israel and to other non-Christian faith communities as well. All conventional missionary approaches toward the Jews, marked as they have been by a sense of superiority in faith on the part of the Christians, must be totally eliminated. What must replace this old-style missionary enterprise is an approach of reverent dialogue. This is not to imply that dialogue is a new missionary technique. Rather it is a recognition on the part of the Christian churches that while they have important contributions to make to humanity's religious understanding, their own faith needs to be deepened and expanded by living contact with the faith of all non-Christian believers, but in a special way with the Jewish tradition which after all formed the context for Christianity's birth.

In the course of the dialogue in which all notions of superiority and all forms of proselytizing are absent, Christians who obviously accept the Christ Event as having a central meaning for the entire human family and consequently a meaning they have a responsibility to share with others will certainly try to express that meaning to their Jewish partners in the dialogue while at the same time listening to explanations of the central aspects of Jewish faith. The direct aim of such dialogue should never be conversion. That in the process of such intense conversation a Christian or a Jew may feel that his/her present faith stance would be enhanced by changing from one faith community to the other is a phenomenon which cannot be completely ruled out. Recognizing the incompleteness of all present faith traditions, personal decisions about conversion should be left to the judgment of individuals and to the mystery of God's grace.

3
Jewish Views of Christianity

Norman Cousins remarked sometime ago that "Christianity and Judaism share one of the great reluctances of history. Both are reluctant to live openly and fully with the fact that Jesus was a Jew. Christian theology has never been able to explain to itself why Jesus should have come out of Judaism. And Judaism has tended to dwell outside the full significance of the Jewishness of Jesus and his vast spiritual role in human history." We have already looked at the Christian side of the question. It would now prove useful to examine briefly the Jewish response to Jesus and Christianity.

In general, it is possible to distinguish at least four major Jewish approaches in the modern era.[80] The first is the one articulated by many Jewish scholars such as Ellis Rivkin, Samuel Sandmel, David Flusser and Geza Vermes. In this perspective Jesus was a Jew, greatly to be admired, who was born of humble stock. He preached an ethical Judaism substantially traditional and in accord with Pharisaic teachings. He aroused the opposition of the Sadducean establishment and was executed by the dominant Roman regime which feared that he might cre-

ate an uprising within subjugated Jewry. It was Paul who
really founded Christianity by fashioning a Christology
that was in large part rooted in non-Jewish religious perspectives.

A second approach, allied to the first, is that advanced by Martin Buber in his famous essay *Two Types
of Faith*.[81] In this work Buber contrasts *pistis* and
emunah. *Emunah*, the faith of Jesus, represents the biblical pattern of faith, while *pistis*, the faith of Paul, followed the Greek idea of faith in propositional form. The
faith of Jesus was broad in character and dealt with the
problems of the entire people Israel. Paul was chiefly in-
terested in the individual and in human salvation through
the mysterious Christ. Buber is also known for his famous reference to Jesus as "my brother."

The writings of Leo Baeck constitute the third major
Jewish perspective on Christianity. Baeck frequently
dealt with Christianity in his essays, the best of which
have been compiled in *Judaism and Christianity*.[82] Rather
than looking for similarities between the two religious
traditions, Baeck considered it his duty to clarify their
basic differences. He thoroughly discussed the problem
presented by Paul's attitude toward Judaism, seeking to
discover the roots of Paul's anti-legalism in the relationship of Paul and the Talmudic idea of "periods" of history. He pointed out that Paul could only have believed in
Jesus as Messiah if he accepted the Talmudic idea that
the "period of Law" had passed and the "period of the
Messiah" had come. Perhaps his most famous and provocative essay was that entitled "Romantic Religion," a
powerful polemic contrasting the weak elements of "romantic" Christianity with the strength of "classic" Judaism.

Finally there is the famous model of Franz Rosenzweig, frequently called the "double covenant" theory, which he unveiled in his classical volume *The Star of Redemption*.[83] Thoroughly grounded in the philosophy of Hegel, Rosenzweig's conception envisions Christianity as Judaism for the Gentiles. Christ in this perspective becomes the necessary intermediary for the Gentiles, still locked in history, to reach God. The Jews, however, the eternal people, do not need Christ because they are already of God.

During the past several years some additional Jewish voices have arisen on the subject of Christianity and its possible role in Jewish self-understanding. Some of these voices have simply called on the Jewish community to begin to address the issue. Others have either offered some theological models for Jewish-Christian co-existence and/or indicated ways in which a study of the Christian faith tradition might positively affect religious values within Judaism. The following are a few examples of such rethinking.

Arthur Cohen has said that Jews must look to Christianity to ransom their faith in the Messiah, and to renew their expectation of the nameless Christ. This, for him, would constitute the center of true Jewish-Christian nexus, what might be called a Jewish-Christian humanism.[84] And a French Jewish writer named Robert Aron, shortly before his recent death, attempted to build a relationship paradigm on the recognition within Judaism of many covenantal moments. He emphasized that the covenantal tradition has two hallmarks. On one hand, there is a continuous movement about them; they perpetually develop without interruption. On the other hand, none of the covenants is ever abolished or outdone by the next one. It is in this perspective that Aron believes a Jew might situate and define the intervention of Jesus in history:

> He appeared at a point in God's history when a new covenant was being drafted—a Catholic covenant in the original sense of the word—the covenant intended for the whole of mankind. Jesus represents a privileged, but difficult moment in the religious history of mankind. . . . Yet he also remains a point of convergence and agreement which in the present state of the world . . . may take on great significance.[85]

Another Jewish author who picks up on the theme of several possible covenants from a Jewish theological perspective is Rabbi Jakob Petuchowski of the Hebrew Union College in Cincinnati. Addressing the 1977 National Workshop on Christian-Jewish Relations in Detroit on the topic of the religious basis for pluralism, Rabbi Petuchowski placed great stress on the rabbinic teaching that God made a covenant with the sons of Noah, that is, with the ancestors of the entire surviving human race. That covenant entailed the observance of seven commandments: the prohibitons of idolatry, sexual immorality, murder, blasphemy, robbery and cruelty to animals, and the one positive commandment about the establishment of courts of law. As Petuchowski sees it, Israel's God stands in a conventual relationship with men and women everywhere. In the encounter with Moses at Mt. Sinai, God incorporated the universal Noahite covenant within the provisions which he specifically gave to the people Israel as their distinctive religious civil constitution. This constitution added to the list of the seven universal Noahite commandments some 606 others, making for a combined total of 613 commandments in the Torah, the ongoing basis for Jewish religious living.

Rabbinic tradition makes it clear, according to Petuchowski, that the covenant on Mt. Sinai in no way obliterated the initial divine covenant with the whole human race. The contrary was true. The non-Jew was expected to be faithful to the demands of the Noahite covenant. The reward for such faithfulness was a share in the world to come. Commenting on the statement from the Prophet Isaiah 26:2 "Open the gates," the rabbis point out that Isaiah did not say that the priests, Levites and Israelites would enter the final kingdom, but rather that the righteous Gentiles would do so. And while the ancient rabbinic tradition never directly confronted this question, Petuchowski feels that there is nothing in Jewish religious belief which would prevent an assumption that, just as God had supplemented the Noahite covenant with the provisions of the Torah as regards Israel, so he likewise supplemented the Noahite covenant with additional convenants in the case of the Gentiles. Petuchowski acknowledges the roles that Christianity and Islam have played in spreading the knowledge of God to the far reaches of the earth. He also shows appreciation for the ideas of both Franz Rosenzweig and James Parkes regarding the Christian-Jewish relationship:

> Like Franz Rosenzweig in the first quarter of the 20th century, I can see the purpose of Christianity to be that of leading the rest of mankind to that relationship with God the Father which Israel has enjoyed ever since Sinai. And like the Anglican priest, Rev. James Parkes, at the present time I can believe in the

contemporaneous validity of the various covenants, so that no one covenant, made by God with a particular segment of the human race, invalidates the others.[86]

A third Jewish voice following to some extent in the direction set forth by Aron and Petuchowski is Rabbi Joshua O. Haberman of the Washington Hebrew Congregation. In an essay on "Universalism and Particularism in Interreligious Dialogue" he argues that the changes in the Christian perception of Judaism over the last decade brought about by official statements from Protestant and Catholic churches and from the research of such theologians as Cornelius Rijk and A. Roy Eckhardt call for a response from the Jewish community. Jews need to begin seriously asking the question, if the old covenant makes them God's people, is the so-called "new" covenant entirely superflous? He insists that the burden of re-defining the relationship between the church and the synagogue does not fall solely on Christianity. Jews must turn their collective attention to the re-examination of the place of the church in Jewish theology. Would it be possible to say, for example, from a Jewish theological perspective that Christians share in certain dimensions of Jewish particularity? In other words, how far do the election and the covenant with Israel apply to Christians as well?

Haberman would pursue these questions by beginning with a reinterpretation of the concept of election so as to include Christian men and women as God's elect without diffusing the uniqueness of Judaism's role in the process of human salvation. Such a recognition would not go counter to the overall Jewish tradition since medieval Jewish philosophy already recognized Christianity as a preparatory stage for the coming universal triumph of monotheism. Haberman also appeals to the thought of the noted Israeli participant in interreligious dialogue Professor R.J. Zwi Werblowsky of the Hebrew University who has insisted that the original Jewish consciousness of election, the awareness by Jews that they are distinct from the Gentile nations, must be understood in terms of *difference*, not in terms of *superiority*.

Haberman feels that the immediate task for Jews in the contemporary dialogue is to start specifying the elements of difference in the election of Israel in a manner that will not rule out the possibility of Christian participation in this election. Is it conceivable for both Judaism and Christianity to claim different but equally valid functions under the notion of a common election? This is a key question for Jews to address. Although Haberman admits that the theological interpretation of Christ as God incarnate remains, for the time being, an irreconcilable difference in the dialogue between Jews and Christians, it is "equally true that the historical Jesus, as a son of Israel, remains the most profound link-in-the flesh between Jews and Christians."[87]

On the Israeli scene where the rethinking of interreligious relations from a Jewish point of view has advanced somewhat further than in Europe or North America through organizations like the Ecumenical Theological Research Fraternity and the Rainbow Dialogue Group several lines of thought are evident. The Orthodox scholar Pinchas Lapide who has engaged in public discussions with Professor Hans Kung as we have seen in Chapter Two takes a more limited approach to the question, concentrating on the more traditional Jewish-Christian issues. Others place the issues more squarely within the dialogue of world religions and the interrelationship of religion and culture.

Lapide speaks of the growing Jewish interest in Jesus as a remarkable development in contemporary Judaism, especially in Israel. He has surveyed some twenty-nine recent books in Hebrew dealing with the significance of Jesus for Jews. He has found these works marked by a common sympathy and love for the Nazarene which would have been unthinkable in previous centuries. In large part, Lapide blames the church for the Jewish inability to confront the reality of Jesus: ". . . if Israel's more famous son has been passed over in silence for so long in Judaism, it is the fault of the church—with its coercive measures, seeking to impose its faith by the sword, which will not work."[88]

Lapide indicates that from a personal standpoint the most significant re-thinking of a Jewish theology of Christianity has revolved around the Christian notions of the Incarnation and the self-abasement of God. For a good part of his life he regarded such notions as totally alien to Judaism. Now he has discovered that there existed germinal traces of both ideas among marginal groups in Judaism as early as the first century before Christ, and became even more frequent in the first and second centuries of the common era. Hence he believes that what most Jews have considered Hellenistic features of the Christian faith in fact owe their origin, at least in part, to trends within Judaism at the time of Christianity's inception. Lapide confesses that it still remains impossible for him to accept the Christian notion of resurrection since it is not suggested by the overall Jewish experience of God. Yet he feels that it is not his place to delimit the possible action of God. His response now to the basic faith tenets of Christianity has changed from a resolute "no" to a state of respectful uncertainty:

. . . unlike the Jewish-Christian controversialists of the last 1800 years, when people turned more and more blatantly from opponents into enemies—I can answer today with a biblical and humble "I do not know"; I would change the angle of vision of our controversy, which has now lasted almost nineteen centuries, from 180°—that is, from a Christian "Yes" in confrontation with a Jewish "no"—to one, if you wish, of 90°—that is, to a Christian "Yes" and a modest Jewish "I do not know."[89]

Lapide goes on to urge joint Christian-Jewish exploration into the life and ministry of Jesus. Such exploration can prove a source of unity for Christians and Jews. Church and synagogue are also united in their understanding that salvation in its fullness still remains a future goal. We both await a coming of the Messiah who will initiate this fullness. Whether this future coming is understood as the first or second coming is really a secondary issue in Lapide's view. Common study and non-judgmental respect for theological differences are what is demanded of Christian and Jews today in our era of religious pluralism.

Professors David Hartman and Shemaryahu Talmon, two Israelis who have had considerable experience in inter-religious dialogue on an international level, take up the Jewish perspective on religious pluralism in a somewhat wider context than Lapide. Hartman believes that the basic problem in inter-religious conflict in past centuries has been caused by the overexaggerated emphasis on *truth*. He insists that *truth* is not the primary religious category in Judaism. He calls for a new pluralistic

spirituality that has radically abandoned the old claims to
absolute truth held by Judaism, Christianity and Islam.
Such abandonment must be all-embracing. The model,
held by some ecumenists, that pluralism is an intermediary position that should be held by a faith group until the
final confirmation of its faith perspective in the endtime,
is totally rejected by Hartman:

> We cannot in some way leap to some eschaton
> and live in two dimensions; to be pluralistic
> now but to be monistic in our eschatological vi-
> sion is bad faith. We have to recognize that ulti-
> mately spiritual monism is a disease. It leads to
> the type of spiritual arrogance that has brought
> bloodshed to history. Therefore we have to re-
> think our eschatology, and rethink the notion of
> multiple spiritual communities and their rela-
> tionship to a monotheistic faith.[90]

Hartman contends that the central problem of pluralism is idolatry. Nearly all religious traditions have
measured idolatry on the basis of what people thought
about God and how they worshiped him. Hartman suggests that the only authentic approach to idolatry today
is to measure it in the way that the Talmud ultimately
does: the crucial thing was not what one thought, but
what one did as a result of what one thought. The Judaeo-Christian heritage will only survive in the future if
Christians and Jews recapture the basic principle given
by God—through the way you live, I will be known. Following this principle to its ultimate will involve the admission by Jews, Christians and Muslims that our different faith stories and religious memories are of equal
stature, abandoning any and all claims for the superiority

of one over the others. This will involve, Hartman admits, a clear break with biblical tradition which he holds in large part responsible for the absolutist claims of religious groups that so often ended up in massive injustice against outsiders. Regarding his own faith tradition, Hartman puts it this way:

> I do not delude myself as to how far I am going when, just as I tell my children that the story of Adam is the story of one man and not the story of the first man, I say that the story of Israel is the story of God's love for a people retained in our family memories. Other people have their own Egypts, their own deserts, their own Sinais, and each one builds from his own; mine is not definite as to what is authentic. I have no criteria as to what is not to count as a person's Egypt or Sinai or desert.[91]

In a presentation to a multilaterial dialogue sponsored by the World Council of Churches' Commission on Dialogue with People of Living Faiths held in Sri Lanka in 1974, Professor Shemaryahu Talmon of the biblical studies department at Hebrew University in Jerusalem laid down several principles for authentic interreligious relations in the context of the search for world community. His first principle is that in formulating proposals for world community each religious tradition must draw upon its particular resources. The emphasis should not be on finding a common basis among all religious traditions. Each religion should bring its own distinctiveness to the common task. Only the conclusions of each group, not the resources for them nor the method of their arrival, should be considered by their brothers and sisters in the dialogue. How a religious group arrives at its proposals for world community is irrelevant to other groups; which resources were used is only of academic interest. What really matters are the conclusions themselves. In this emphasis Talmon appears to be focusing on the same principle advocated by Hartman, namely, that the only legitimate way of judging another group is by how it acts on what it thinks.

Talmon's second operative principle shows some disagreement with Hartman's stance. Talmon admits that many religious traditions and ideologies, especially in the Western World, harbor in varying degrees dreams of universal acceptance of their views either by force or persuasion:

> The utopian views of Christianity and Islam have traditionally envisioned the ideal state of mankind as the embracing by all humans of their respective prophets of dogma. Judaism, at the very least, looks forward to the obliteration of idolatry, and the universal acceptance of the One God and his moral code. Marxism strives for domination by the proletariat and the establishment of a classless society based on its dialectical materialism. If such ultimate aims are denied, we are false to these individual outlooks.[92]

Talmon then poses the ultimate question. How can the various faith communities work together to produce world community if each really wants the others to acknowledge its spiritual truth, if Christians want all Jews eventually to accept Jesus, if Muslims continue with the goal of wanting all peoples to recognize Muhammad as the supreme prophet, if Jews continue their tradition of viewing other religions as basically idolatrous, and if Marxists continue to see religions as a fundamental obstacle to the realization of their utopian vision? What is needed from all religions and ideologies, Talmon suggests, is a common decision that, having laid their respective eschatological goals in the open, they will look upon the task of building world community as essentially non-eschatological, or, at best, pre-eschatological. Tied in with this must be a resolve that even if world community represents, according to the insights of a particular religious or ideological group a pre-eschatological state, such world community must never become the occasion for activist eschatological realization and for the proselytization that it implies.

Talmon recognizes that he is asking a great deal from those religious traditions and ideologies for whom the achievement of the endtime is a central doctrine and the motivation for concrete action. But he insists that unless such self-restraint becomes the rule, the quest for world community will be stillborn. In this approach Talmon is not as relativistic as Hartman. He does not call for the abandonment of eschatological truth claims which Hartman sees as essential for the development of authentic religious pluralism on a worldwide scale.

Another Jewish approach to Christianity today comes from Rabbi Irving Greenberg, a respected scholar who has been deeply involved in study of the Nazi holocaust. He feels strongly that both Christianity and Judaism are placed on a new footing by reason of the Auschwitz experience. The overall significance of the holocaust in the contemporary Jewish-Christian relationship theologically has been invalidated by the holocaust. For him both Jewish and Christian theology today must incorpo-

incorporate the holocaust as a central orienting event in the expression of their respective faith traditions. Auschwitz stands as radical counter-testimony for both Judaism and Christianity. The magnitude of suffering and the evident worthlessness of human life which mark the Nazi experiment radically contradict basic affirmations of human value and divine concern in both religions. Failure to grapple with this evil will turn both Judaism and Christianity "into empty, Pollyanna assertions, credible only because believers ignore the realities of human history."[93]

Greenberg is convinced that both Christianity and Judaism need to look upon the holocaust as a new revelatory event. Their theological formulation in our day cannot ignore its implications. For him the very anguish and harsh judgments which Auschwitz casts on the Christian church open the possibility for freeing the basic gospel of love (which Greenberg profoundly respects) from becoming mired in evil and hatred. Since Greenberg also believes that the holocaust demolishes much of the grandeur of Western secular culture, he sees an urgent need for religious influence in our contemporary world if human life is to be respected on all levels. Both Judaism and Christianity have an important role to play. But both require significant purification, though Greenberg sees the burden as falling more heavily on Christianity because of its contributions to the Nazi atrocities.

Creating new theological models for the Jewish-Christian relationship in a limited sense is not Greenberg's chief concern. Rather he believes that the destruction that Auschwitz brought to both religion and secular culture necessitates that Christians and Jews begin both to probe their own faith tradition and experience and to work cooperatively in recreating human life, in finding

faith anew in our day, and in recreating the image of
God. Only in this context will the discussion of new models for the relationship between church and synagogue
have any value or purpose.

The holocaust has also served as the basis for another Jewish scholar's attitude toward Christianity and
its importance for Judaism today. Dr. Eliezer Berkovits
of the Hebrew Theological College in Skokie, Illinois, has
emerged as the most outspoken Jewish critic of Christian-Jewish dialogue in our time. This Orthodox scholar
simply feels that Judaism has absolutely nothing to gain
from study of or contact with the Christian church. In
fact, in some ways he looks upon such dialogue as an in-
sult to the memory of the six million Jews who died during the holocaust. He likewise is of the opinion that
Christianity is dying as a religious tradition, that we are
now in the post-Christian era. So why should Judaism
bother with a church on its deathbed. He remains convinced that there is no way Christianity will ever overcome its theological anti-Semitism which he finds rooted
in the teachings of the New Testament. This anti-Semitism is satanic and pagan at its source and has been responsible for the destruction of fundamental human value in society on a worldwide scale. His writings on the
dialogue are characterized by bluntness of the following
sort:

> Christianity has practiced genocide upon the
> Jewish people for many centuries. Without that
> Christian practice, and its self-righteous justifi-
> cation, the gas chambers and crematoria of
> Auschwitz and Treblinka would not have been
> possible. The theme is not how to live in peace
> with each other, notwithstanding credal differ-

ences. The fundamental theme is not religion
and dogma, but inhumanity and barbarism of
an intensity, consistency and duration unique in
human history. Before anything else one has to
face the truth of Christian criminality against
the Jewish people.[94]

While both Greenberg and Berkovits take the holocaust
as their point of departure for present-day Jewish-Christian relations, Berkovits shows little of the sense of Jewish self-purification that Greenberg insists Auschwitz demands of Jewish theology. Also, unlike Greenberg, he
sees little hope that Christianity will purge itself of historic anti-Semitism nor does he admit that a cleansed Christian church needs to play a central role alongside a re-
formed Judaism in preserving the dignity of human life in
modern culture. The only likely result from any intensive
encounter with Christianity for Jews is the corruption of
their own religious spirit.

Rabbi Henry Siegman is another Jewish voice in the
dialogue whose views have had significant influence. In
his former capacity as Executive Director of the Synagogue Council of America this Orthodox rabbi has par-
ticipated in conversations with Christian churches na-
tionally and internationally. Siegman has generally
maintained the position that the dialogue should concen-
trate on more practical social questions rather than on
theological questions. Nonetheless, he is strong in his call
for greater Jewish self-examination regarding Christianity. In his mind Judaism has an inner need to come to
terms with how a meaningful pluralism might impact on
the Jewish religious tradition. Jews have been somewhat
less than daring in launching a process of self-reflection

in this regard. Rabbi Siegman acknowledges that the memory of Jewish persecution at the hands of Christians complicates the attempt by Jews to take seriously their own classical affirmations of the religious worth of the Christian religion. But Jews do not of necessity compromise their religious integrity by admitting, in line with the classical Jewish tradition, that Christians who live a good and decent life do so not despite but because of the Christianity they profess. A more authentic and developed Jewish response to Christianity is on the horizon. It will attain further growth in the measure that Jewish people regain a measure of self-confidence and spiritual poise. A secure and flourishing State of Israel will without doubt speed up this process.

Siegman raises questions regarding the call by many of his Jewish colleagues that Christian theology grant Judaism an equal status with the church. This would imply a counter affirmation by Jews about Christianity which he does not feel they can make with integrity. His model for the church-synagogue relationship is one in which each faith tradition maintains a belief in its ultimate superiority. Hence, Siegman does not share in the viewpoint advocated by Hartman nor perhaps even in the stand of Talmon:

> As a believing Jew, I affirm that Judaism is the "truest" religion. That affirmation is part of what makes me a believing Jew, and I do not expect Christians to be offended by it. Conversely, I cannot be offended by parallel affirmations of faith made by Christians—or by Muslims, Hindus, or Buddhists, for that matter. To insist that Christians may not entertain such

> beliefs about their own faith is to cut the
> ground from under the Jewish position. It is to
> say that Jews can talk only to those who are less
> secure in their own faith than we are in ours.[95]

For Siegman, Judaism constitutes a denial of the central
Christian mystery and the consequent notion of salvation. It is hardly legitimate for Judaism, therefore, to utter such a denial and then demand that Christian theology be recast to make room for the validity of Judaism.
In fact, Christian claims about the church as the fulfillment of Judaism parallel the traditional Jewish conviction that Judaism is the completion of Christianity, phe-
nomenologically if not chronologically.

Judaism can profit greatly spiritually and intellec-
tually from serious and honest dialogue across faith lines.
What Judaism does not need from other religious traditions, however, and what no other religion can in fact
give it, is a validation of its own central faith affirmations. This can come only from within Jewish life and
thought, not from without. It in no way downgrades
Christianity for a Jew to state that Christian recognition
of the non-abrogation of the Sinaitic covenant adds no
significant meaning to Jewish theology.

Without specifying just what it is that Judaism
might learn from the religious dialogue with Christians,
Siegman seems to be making the kind of general suggestion which Rabbi Irving Greenberg has tried to specify to
some extent. Greenberg believes that the new Jewish-
Christian encounter can significantly advance the internal development of Judaism. In the first place, it may aid
Jews in overcoming what Greenberg has termed "the
hostility-cancer" in Jewry. To the degree past persecution
has legitimated a hostility or stereotyping of Gentiles,

and to the extent that this has become an important component of Jewish self-identity, the vanishing of this antagonism toward Gentiles because of contacts in the dialogue may lead to a Jewish self-definition in which voluntary choice and love become more prominent. "This would end," says Greenberg, "the tragic distortion of the Jew's identity being partly the definition I am against the other."[96]

In a similar way Judaism may come to see new value in some of its own sacramental traditions. The development of the rabbinic tradition, while wholly legitimate in Greenberg's eyes, had the side-effect of shifting the center of equilibrium in Jewish religious life away from the sacramental dimensions. The end result of this has been the neglect of the role that grace plays in Jewish faith. A more subtle and meaningful balance of grace and personal responsibility may perhaps emerge within contemporary Judaism as a result of more in-depth exposure to the sacramental dimensions in Christianity through dialogical interchange.

From the above survey it should be clear that Jewish re-thinking of the contribution that Christianity might make to its religious self-understanding is in its infancy. A growing number of Jewish scholars do see a potential contribution, though some continue to maintain that Christianity really has nothing to add to Jewish insights about human religiosity. In general, Jewish scholars have not gone as far as Christians in the reformulation of their stance regarding the other. Israeli scholars have in some ways forged ahead of European and American Jews in this respect although one must not overestimate the influence of these scholars on over-all Jewish thinking in Israel. In addition to the reformulation of the Jewish attitude toward Christianity, Jewish scholars are still behind

Christians generally in formulating theological principles
for religious pluralism. It needs to be recognized in all
fairness, however, that this may be the first generation of
Jews who have religious freedom, and in Israel the majority status, to contemplate such a task. For many centuries
Jews were simply and rightly concerned about staying
alive and maintaining religious survival.

While acknowledging the difficulties that Jews face
in trying to take Christianity seriously in light of the history of the church's anti-Semitism, it is important for
Christian scholars to encourage their Jewish colleagues to
advance their re-thinking of the Jewish-Christian relationship. And this reformulation must go beyond some of
the classical positions which we have examined. There is
some validity in the often voiced Jewish claim that such a
process is not as central to Judaism as it is to Christianity. Judaism, it is argued, can develop an integral self-
definition without direct reference to Christianity, while
Christianity, of necessity, must include Judaism as a reference point in its self-definition. This line of argument,
however, too easily overlooks the fact that Jesus arose
and ministered within the context of the Jewish community. In addition, applying to Judaism the same principle
that many would make mandatory for Christianity, it is
legitimate to say that Judaism's understanding of the
spiritual nature of the human person remains incomplete
without some sharing of insights from Christianity and
other world religions.

With regard to the more traditional Jewish approaches to Christianity outlined at the beginning of this
chapter, the following observations seem appropriate.
The first approach which looks upon Jesus as a respect-
able Jewish preacher and considers Paul the actual
founder of Christianity contains elements relative to the

basic Jewishness of Jesus and his connections with the Pharisaic movement that certainly need underscoring. But in the long run, in not grappling with the divinity aspect of the Christ symbol, it weakens Christianity and overlooks what constitutes the ultimate uniqueness of Christianity and its greatest potential contributions to the dialogue of world religions. Also, the distinction made between the religion of Jesus and Pauline religion needs to be rethought. There is a sense in which the evangelist John and the mature Paul can be looked upon as the fathers of Christianity. We have also seen how E.P. Sanders has stressed the difference in form between Pauline religion and the rabbinic milieu in which Jesus worked and taught. But, nonetheless, the developed Christologies of John and Paul owed more to Judaism that this school of thought has admitted and were directly rooted in realities which arose in the teachings and ministry of Jesus himself.

The positions taken by Buber and Baeck were too exclusively colored by their contact with a highly selective group of Protestant theologians and exegetes. While some of their observations may be correct with respect to the version of Christianity with which they were in direct contact, they failed to do justice to the broad range of Christian expression.

The Rosenzweig model, despite its initial attractiveness, must be rejected for two reasons. First, in reversing the traditional sequence, it makes Judaism the final and complete religion and Christianity the inferior religion still striving for completion. Rosenzweig speaks of the complementariness of the two religions, but it is one of unequals in his scheme. The objection here would not be too dissimilar to the one voiced in connection with the Christian use of Romans 9–11 as a relational model. Secondly, in basically removing the Jewish people from the historical process, Rosenzweig does violence to one of the basic hallmarks of the Jewish spirit—its rootedness in the flow of history which is the locus of human salvation.

We can say with all honesty that from a Christian perspective Judaism has not yet come up with a relationship model that is genuinely attractive. The reflections of Irving Greenberg on the holocaust will certainly have to influence such a model. The suggestion of multiple convenants by Aron and Petukowski also points in the right direction. Talmon and Hartman likewise make significant contributions though the latter relativizes both faith traditions too much. Judaism needs to search more deeply into its own self-identity and then study the unique features of Christianity to ascertain in what ways its faith perspective may be modified and deepened. In so doing it likely will undergo more of a transformation than someone like Siegman seems willing to allow.

Before concluding this chapter on Jewish views of Christianity, some comments are in order regarding the view of the church in Jewish educational materials. Overall, the results in this regard were far more positive than those obtained from the Yale and St. Louis studies on the Christian portrait of Judaism. The Dropsie College analysis of Jewish texts, undertaken during the same period as the Christian studies, revealed minimal prejudice in mainline Jewish materials. If a criticism can be made of the materials, it would be over their silence regarding the Christian tradition. The excuse given for this is generally that Judaism can be taught without direct reference to Christianity unlike Christianity's inherent need to refer to Judaism in its self-definition. While this explanation may be inadequate for many Christians in the dialogue today, nonetheless Christians need to applaud the relative lack of stereotyping that the Dropsie studies showed and contrast this situation with the results from Yale and St. Louis.

At a national conference on teaching faith without prejudice held at St. Louis University in 1975, Dr. Max Nadel of the American Association of Jewish Education cited statements concerning Jesus, Christians and Christianity from textual materials currently in use in Jewish religious schools. According to his findings there is a serious effort afoot on the part of Jewish textbook writers to present Christianity and Christians in non-stereotypic and even sympathetic terms.[97]

Perhaps even more comprehensive work has been done with respect to the image of Christianity in Israeli textbooks. Professor Pinchas Lapide has studied ten important Hebrew-language texts and found them quite positive in tone. In addition, in 1970, the Israeli ministry of education formulated an official account of early Christianity by means of a thirty-five page booklet designed for use in the seventh grade. The booklet's four chapters place Jesus within the Jewish context of the period, outline his influence and appeal, speak about the messianic aspects of Jesus' ministry, and report his confrontation with the authorities which led to his condemnation and crucifixion.

Lapide's general conclusions regarding the textbooks he examined run as follows. In the first place, Jesus is never held responsible for subsequent Christian hatred of Jews nor is there any attempt to project later Christian history onto the teachings of Jesus. Secondly, the texts take for granted the Jewishness of Jesus though they differ in their interpretation of his historical role. Some materials portray him as a messianic pretender or an apocalyptic preacher, others present him as a moral teacher or a seducer of the populace, while a few show him as a patriotic rebel against the yoke of Roman authority. Whatever the portrait, however, almost all of the texts treat his suffering and death at the hands of the Romans with considerable empathy. Finally, though a few passages in the materials speak of Jesus as having diverged from the normative Judaism of the period, references to his loyalty to Jewish teaching, to the rootedness of his teachings in the Hebrew Scriptures and to his basic Jewish ethos predominate by far.[98]

4
Jesus and the
Pharisaic Tradition

The third major area of distortion of Judaism uncovered in the St. Louis textbook studies was the depiction of the Pharisees. It is the one which has shown the least improvement during the decade since II Vatican although recently there are some promising beginnings. For one, the 1975 Vatican Guidelines on Catholic-Jewish Relations specifically mentioned the image of the Pharisees as an aspect of Judaism that requires much correction in Christian education and preaching. And the 1973 statement from the French episcopal commission on relations with Jews spoke to the issue with great clarity:

> Contrary to established ways of thinking, it must be emphasized that Pharisaic doctrine is not opposed to that of Christianity. The Pharisees sought to make the law come alive in every Jew, by interpreting its commandments in such a way as to adapt them to the various spheres of life. Contemporary research has shown that the Pharisees were no more strangers to the inner-

most meaning of the law than were the masters
of the Talmud.[99]

The document goes on to say that Jesus did battle with
only certain groups within the Pharisaic movement. And
even in these situations they fought with one another
about the interpretation of the Mosaic Law and Jewish
tradition because of the similarity of their basic posture
toward religious living. It was for the most part a fierce
"in house" struggle. Jesus never condemned the Pharisaic movement as a whole, the document insists, for the
empty formalism and spiritually vapid legalism that
Christians usually associate with Pharisaism.

Additionally, some Christian scholars have begun to
seriously study Second Temple Judaism, Pharisaism in
particular. E.P. Sanders is a prime example. And the
writings of such pioneer scholars on Pharisaism as R.
Travers Herford and George Foote Moore and of more
recent ones like Ellis Rivkin, Jacob Neusner, David
Flusser, Louis Finkelstein and Asher Finkel are beginning to reach a wider Christian audience. Dr. Charlotte
Klein has shown in her study of anti-Judaism in Christian theology referred to earlier that the influence of Herford and Moore in particular has resulted in a more sympathetic presentation of the Judaism of Jesus' day among
Anglo-American theologians and Scripture scholars than
is the case in continental Europe.

Yet, with the virtual elimination of the deicide
charge from mainline Christian educational materials, it
is fair to say that the stereotyping of the Pharisees constitutes the most significant distortion of ancient Judaism
remaining in the Christian consciousness. For most believing Christians the Pharisees remain the shady charac-
ters portrayed in the musical *Godspell*. Dr. Eugene Fish-

er, in his update of the St. Louis textbook studies, confirms this continuing difficulty with the portrait of the Pharisees. Of the ten categories of Christian-Jewish relations he examined, the Pharisaic category showed the most distortion for both primary and secondary materials. His remarks on this situation are most pertinent:

> Throughout the series, the Pharisees are paint-
> ed in dark, evil colors. The danger here lies not
> only in a distortion of history. Deeper is the fact
> that negative traits ascribed to the Pharisees are
> likely to be imputed to the Jews as a whole by
> the uncritical reader or teacher. Legalism, hy-
> pocrisy and craftiness are all stereotypes of
> Jews which owe their origins to a negative por-
> trait of the Pharisees.[100]

The removal of this distorted portrait of the Pharisees is vital both for the sake of the dialogue and in order to enhance the process of Christian self-renewal. It is important for the sake of the dialogue since most contemporary expressions of Judaism, despite their profound variations, fundamentally are rooted in the Pharisaic-rabbinic movement's approach to religion which resulted in genuinely revolutionary changes during the Second Temple period. So to negatively portray the Pharisees is in a real way to attack the centrality of modern Judaism.

But it is likewise crucial for the church to become better acquainted with Pharisaism as it pursues the task of renewing its life as a faith community; for the Pharisaic movement formed the context of the teachings of Jesus and the early church in such crucial areas as ethics, the notion of God, liturgy, ministry and institutional structure. For Christians to acquire a proper grasp of the New

Testament it is essential that they understand the principal themes of Pharisaic-rabbinic Judaism. Authentic renewal within the contemporary church cannot be brought about without an appreciation of the significance of the Pharisaic revolution and all it meant for the style of religious living in the period in which Christianity was born.

As with most scholarly questions, there is not complete agreement about the Pharisaic movement in every detail. Professors Jacob Neusner[101] and Ellis Rivkin[102] who are the principal figures presently investigating Pharisaism do not agree completely on the origins of the movement nor on its basic posture at the time of Jesus. Rivkin, for example, would see the Pharisees as a more open, revolutionary group in Jesus' day while Neusner is inclined to believe that they had become a more elitist table-fellowship by this period. Part of the problem arises from the difficulty in dating Pharisaic materials. All our extant Pharisaic materials come from later documents and there is a measure of uncertainty as regards which ideas can be legitimately projected back into the time in which Jesus was alive. Additionally, there is considerable disagreement between Neusner and Rivkin over the reliability of the historian Josephus who reports extensively about the activities of the Pharisees. Rivkin relies on Josephus as a prime source while Neusner tends to discount him.

It is not possible in this volume to go into the discussion about the Pharisaic movement with any thoroughness. Running through the various scholarly viewpoints are some common trends which can be summarized in the following manner.

At the heart of the Pharisaic revolution lay a new perspective on the God-human person relationship—one far more personal and intimate than any previous movement within Judaism had envisioned. This changed perception was so profound that the Pharisees felt obliged to devise new titles for God and to restrict the old names to quotations from the Hebrew Scriptures. One of the principal names they applied to God was "Father." This term may not sound very revolutionary to modern ears. But, as developed by the Pharisees, the Father-Son imagery reveals a consciousness of a new intimacy between God and the individual person. This new sense of divine-human intimacy ultimately tore holes in the intermediary/hereditary elite system that formed the core of the Sadducean Temple priesthood approach to religion. Every person, no matter who he or she might be, had such standing before God so as to be able to relate to him directly without need for intermediaries. Thus there were no longer any grounds for preserving a select class of people who, because they were born into priestly families, automatically held a distinct status in the eyes of God and were the only ones who could communicate with Adonai. Inevitably this "spiritual" transformation led to a complete reshaping of the liturgical, ministerial and institutional life of Second Temple Judaism.

Viewing themselves as the heirs of the prophetic tradition, and transformed by the new intimate, personal link with God, the Pharisees introduced basic changes into the ongoing pattern of Jewish existence with the goal of translating prophetic ideals into daily lived realities. These changes had a far-reaching influence on the teachings of Jesus and Paul and on the structures of the early church.

One of the most fundamental changes initiated by the Pharisees was the shift in focus from the Temple to the synagogue as the central religious institution in Jewish life. The Temple was looked upon primarily as the house of God. The synagogue in contrast became the house of the people of God. The nuance is crucial. The Temple was essentially a place where cult and sacrifice were offered. The synagogue, on the other hand, strove to meet the total needs of the people—prayer, study, justice. Christians have frequently overlooked the fact that the word "church" basically stems from the word "synagogue". So as Christians go about the process of rethinking the contour of the central religious institution of their faith, they can learn a great deal from a study of the Pharisaic conception of the synagogue and how it differed from the Temple model. The II Vatican Council after all placed great emphasis on the notion of the church as the people of God.

The second innovative feature of the Pharisaic revolution was the person of the rabbi who gradually replaced the Temple priest as the central religious figure in Judaism. The rabbi was essentially a lay person, a minister who had no specific liturgical functions.

A position of community leadership came to a rabbi only after demonstration of a living knowledge of Torah, both in synagogal debates and even more importantly by healing people and showing mercy in the marketplace. Jesus basically followed the rabbinic pattern in his own ministry, a fact clearly acknowledged in the New Testament. Thus an examination of the Pharisaic changeover from Temple priest to rabbi will prove of immense value for the continuing debate over the nature of Christian ministry.

A third crucial innovation stemming from the Pharisaic period was the shifting of the ordinary liturgical life of the people from the Temple to a home-meal setting where the father of the family or the head of a Pharisaic brotherhood presided. The significance of this Pharisaic change is to be found in its abandonment of the sacrificial concept of liturgy and its attempt to place worship within a setting of natural community celebration. Since it is likely that Jesus presided at the so-called Last Supper in his capacity as head of a Pharisaic brotherhood (i.e., his apostles), exposure to the Pharisaic approach to liturgy would significantly aid a Christian's perception of what the Eucharist was and ought to be in the life of the Christian community.

Another major feature of Pharisaism was its development of the notion of oral Torah. Oral Torah was seen by the Pharisees as a way of opening the written Torah to continuous development and application. It may be argued that oral Torah lies at the root of the Catholic and Orthodox notions of tradition as a source of revelation. Unfortunately, unlike the Pharisees, Christians have often become "pharisaic" in their approach to tradition, looking upon it as a restricting tool rather than one for fresh development. Investigation of the oral Torah concept can help revive among Christians an authentic appreciation for tradition as a source of revelation. It will also aid them in seeing that Torah in Judaism is not the same as the overriding Western notion of law as a restrictive force, but signifies rather the basic responses that people of faith need to make to the experience of God's presence.

A fifth important component of the Pharisaic revolution as viewed from a Christian perspective is the notion of the resurrection of the individual person. The New Testament mentions resurrection as a major point of contention between the Pharisees who believed in it and the Sadducees who did not. It was really the Pharisees who introduced into religious language and perception a belief that would take on cardinal importance in Christian theology. An understanding of how resurrection was a natural outflow of the Pharisaic perception of the heightened dignity of the individual person would add considerably to the theology of death and dying that is attracting widespread attention in today's world. As developed by Pharisaism and early Christianity, the doctrine of resurrection constituted a profound statement about the uniqueness and dignity of the individual person.

An examination of Pharisaic ethics will also reveal close parallels to the moral stance espoused by Jesus, with the Sermon on the Mount serving as a prime example of their correlation. Likewise the Pharisees sought to undermine the political power of the Jerusalem priesthood over the Jewish population, an effort supported by Jesus in his own ministry—most dramatically through his invasion of the Temple precincts. This action by no stretch of the imagination can be interpreted as merely a protest against empty ritual. It was meant as a judgment on the Temple system as such.

As a conglomerate, the Pharisaic structures and ideas point to a new closeness between God and the human person. The Pharisees as such were probably not ready to grant the direct link between humanity and divinity that eventually emerged in Christianity. The gulf between humanity and divinity remains deep in Judaism till this day as someone like the great modern interpreter of Judaism Rabbi Abraham Heschel has clearly shown. We have seen, however, that Professor Lapide has uncovered some "incarnational" ideas on the fringes of first century A.D. Judaism. Nonetheless, mainstream Judaism was not prepared to incorporate any such notions though it might be suggested that the Pharisees seemed to be heading in that direction. The disagreement between Ju-

69854

daism and Christianity over the issue of the Incarnation remains very deep indeed. But an understanding of the Pharisaic basis of Christology may make passage of the gulf at some future date at least thinkable.

It was out of this Pharisaic context that Rabbi Jesus emerged and developed his ministry. A prime focus of that ministry was emphasizing the utter dignity of each man and woman. It is somewhat immaterial whether we actually call Jesus a Pharisee. Professor Paul Winter in his volume *On the Trial of Jesus* clearly labels Jesus a Pharisee. Jesus' ethical teaching accords perfectly with the Pharisaic posture. Regarding eschatological outlooks Winter feels that Jesus betrays early Pharisaic attitudes, prior to the wars with Rome, when eschatology was more prominent in Pharisaic teaching than it was in the later tannaitic age:

> . . . Jesus of Nazareth . . . might have been representative of pre-rabbinical Pharisaism not only in his ethical teaching, but also in his eschatology. Of course, this is not to be taken to imply that Jesus did not formulate his views in his own individual fashion. It is the general tenor which corresponds with the Pharisaic pattern; on the ethical side quite obviously, and on the eschatological conceivably. . . . In the whole of the New Testament we are unable to find a single historically reliable instance of religious differences between Jesus and members of the Pharisaic guild, let alone evidence of a mortal conflict.[103]

Winter insists that the violent opposition between Jesus and "the Pharisees" depicts a state of affairs which had come about only several decades after the crucifixion when the early church and rabbinic tradition had already gone their separate ways. But even in the latter part of the first century of the common era when the theological claims advanced by the Christian-Jewish sect were already well-differentiated from the beliefs of the more moderate wing of Pharisaic Jews, Christianity and Pharisaic Judaism stood closer together than either of them did to the Sadducees.

Not all scholars would accept Winter's attribution of Pharisaic status to Jesus. In a way it is immaterial whether we classify Jesus as an actual Pharisee or not. What we can say without hesitation is that the major ideas of the Pharisaic revolution exercised a profound influence on his teachings and the shape of his ministry. He stood much closer to Pharisaism than to any other Jewish movement of the period.

Having established the intimate link between Jesus and the Pharisaic movement we are forced of course to confront the apparent hostility between him and the Pharisees in the New Testament. Paul Winter has already suggested one answer to the dilemma. The conflicts as recorded in the gospels represent later additions which reflect tensions between church and synagogue in the latter portion of the first century rather than actual hostile encounters between Jesus and the Pharisees of his day. Another possible explanation arises from an examination of the way the Talmud handles the Pharisaic movement. According to the Israeli scholar David Flusser the Talmud lists seven types of people who call themselves Pharisees.[104] Five of these are described in a negative way in the Talmud which contains the writings of the Pharisaic rabbis themselves. And even among the two "positive" types, what Flusser terms the Pharisees of awe (or veteran Pharisees) and the Pharisees of love, there were serious disagreements. The Pharisees with whom Jesus was most closely identified were likely the love Pharisees. The gospel condemnations, even if they should actually reflect the words of Jesus himself, are not necessarily global accusations against the entire Pharisaic movement. They were most probably directed against certain groups of people who considered themselves Pharisees but were not living up to the religious ideals the love Pharisees considered crucial to the integrity of the Pharisaic ideal. This explanation has the advantage of requiring no postulation of later additions to the gospel text.

Also to be noted in this connection is the research of Ellis Rivkin.[105] He has found that the term "Pharisee" was regarded as a negative term by the Pharisees themselves. They preferred to be known as the scribes or the wise ones. "Pharisee" was used by the Sadducees, the opponents of the Pharisees, in a derogatory fashion. One of its chief meanings was "heretic." Jesus and/or the later Christian community may have picked up this derogatory usage and applied it in a sarcastic fashion to those members of the Pharisaic movement who appeared to them as "whited sepulchres" in comparison to authentic Pharisaic teaching.

Looking at Jesus then as basically a part of the overall Pharisaic movement, it is necessary to ask whether there are significant differences between him and the general Pharisaic creed. Winter, as was noted above, claims there are not. This position appears somewhat extreme. David Flusser, for example, who has studied the New Testament as thoroughly as any contemporary Jewish scholar, sees at least one unique quality in Jesus' message. He feels that the moral approach to God and people presented in Jesus' teachings is unique and incomparable:

According to the teaching of Jesus you have to
love the sinners, while according to Judaism
you have not to hate the wicked. It is important
to note the positive love even toward the enemies of Jesus' personal message. We do not find
this doctrine in the New Testament outside of
the words of Jesus himself. . . .In Judaism hatred is practically forbidden. But love of the en-
emy is not prescribed.[106]

Following out the notion of the basic dignity of the individual person which was so central to both Pharisaism
and the message of Jesus, we find Jesus eating with the
tax collectors and harlots (the dregs of the society of the
day), constantly preaching reconciliation, and in times of
conflict tending to take the side of the individual. This
last theme in Jesus' ministry is underscored by James
Parkes in his interpretation of the hostility between Jesus
and "the Pharisees" in the pages of the New Testament.
In the gospel of Mark which refrains from the wholesale
condemnation of the Pharisees found in Matthew, their
confrontation occurs as a result of Jesus' healing on the
Sabbath and his disciples plucking corn on the day of
rest. The Pharisees, Parkes says, were concerned with the
survival of the Jewish community in the midst of secular-
ist and assimilationist tendencies among some Jews.

Observance of the Sabbath was a key element for
maintaining the community consciousness the Pharisees
felt to be an indispensable ingredient for Jewish survival.
Jesus also shared their concern about Jewish communal
survival. He said he had not come to destroy Torah but
to bring it to perfection (a clear rejection of the assimilationist position). But while in this conflict both sides
agreed with the principle that "the Sabbath was made for

man, not man for the Sabbath," Jesus chose to carry the Pharisaic principle of the utter and unqualified dignity of each person to its ultimate conclusion. His healing of a diseased hand on the Sabbath was in itself not a crucial issue, according to Parkes, but it was done deliberately by Jesus "as an assertion of the primacy of each man as person."[107]

Yet Parkes insists that Jesus never attempted, as far as we know, to discuss with the Pharisees how to achieve a reconciliation between the need of an individual person and the need of the community. Such reconciliation, says Parkes, cannot be achieved by any simple formula. Jesus never tried to bridge this gap between his own vision and the legitimate Pharisaic concern for the preservation of the community: "Within the divinely chosen community he proclaimed the divine concern with each man as person. It is for men to hold the two in a continuously destroyed and continuously recreated balance. Jesus did not attempt to resolve the tension for us. He challenged us only to recognize that it existed."[108]

So Parkes is saying that both Jesus and the Pharisees were right. It is essential to realize, according to Parkes, that the Pharisees could no more have simply accepted Jesus' teaching than he could have given in to theirs. This is a crucial point, for it opens the door for constructing a model of the Jewish-Christian relationship that gives some credence to the Jewish rejection of Christianity other than unbelief and also opens the way for recognizing that each faith community has emphasized distinct but complementary aspects of the God-human person relationship.

Another example of Jesus' stress on the dignity of the human person, and another instance of a clash with the Jewish leadership, is to be found in the issue of the forgiveness of sins. For even the "liberal" Pharisees, it was unthinkable that anyone but the Father could forgive sins. But Jesus says "no," goes ahead and forgives sins, and even transfers this power to his followers. Viewed within the theological context of the time, this action by Jesus constitutes a significant assertion of the dignity of the human person and the divine power that rests within him or her.

Jesus also carries on the Pharisaic tradition of the resurrection of the dead spoken of above. There is not a great deal that Jesus added to this most important Pharisaic belief. The only noticeable difference would be that the Pharisees insisted, in keeping with their community orientation, that no individual would arise until the Messianic Age since no one could enjoy full salvation until the community has reached its total development.

Some New Testament scholars have suggested that one of the most distinguishing characteristics of Jesus' ministry is his continual concern for the "people of the land" as they are called by the gospel writers. These were the poor and the social outcasts of his day. There is some danger of overexaggerating this point. But undeniably, in keeping with the general thrust of his public life as we have outlined it, Jesus showed a special regard for the situation of these people. There is a real sense in which he identified with their condition. If the Neusner perspective on the Pharisees as having become a more restricted table fellowship in Jesus' day is validated, then there is a significant contrast here. But at the moment, the most we can say is that Jesus pre-occupied himself more with the situation of the "people of the land" than the general run of Pharisees and he worried more intensely about the injustice that was their lot.

Those features of Jesus' ministry that placed him apart from the general Pharisaic stance all point in the direction of later Christological developments in the church. Jesus lived out in his preaching and healing the Incarnational theology later articulated by Paul and John in particular. There is an obvious connection with Pharisaism in this theology. But there is also a qualitative difference. In the work of Jesus which was a reflection of his intense experience of God as Father which Schillebeeckx perceptively emphasizes, the early church came to appreciate a new dimension of the God-human person relationship. God had become incarnated in humanity. It is this profound conviction that would ultimately lead to the creation of Christianity as a distinct religious tradition despite its continuing, deep ties to the Jewish religious tradition.

5
Christian Theology
and the Jewish
Land Tradition

There are two issues that must occupy a central place in the Christian-Jewish dialogue today, and they are interrelated: the holocaust and Israel. A few Jewish writers, borrowing Christian terms, have described them in terms of death-resurrection. The St. Louis studies, as well as the Yale studies, found little mention of these two consciousness-forming realities in contemporary Jewish life. Thus the image of Judaism was distorted in this regard by omission rather than by direct stereotyping. In the textbook series studied by Dr. Fisher there was considerable improvement with respect to the holocaust which he says was handled with great sensitivity by most of the textbook writers. Regarding Israel, however, the results are not much different from the St. Louis findings. Both topics need further airing in the dialogue if we are ever to reach a point of mutual understanding between Jews and Christians.[109]

We turn first to the question of Israel and its links with the historic Jewish land tradition. It has become evident to anyone even reasonably close to world Jewry that Israel has assumed a primary identification role for the contemporary Jewish community. Hence, in keeping with the call of the 1975 Vatican Guidelines for Catholic-Jewish Relations, it is absolutely necessary for Christian men and women to come to understand how Jews define themselves with respect to modern Israel. While a variety of perspectives on Israel will likely emerge from such an investigation, a central motif will clearly appear. Despite the differences of viewpoint on Israel among present-day Jews, virtually all hold Israel to be at the very center of their contemporary self-identity. One Jewish scholar in an address to a Christian audience several years ago said that "for us Jews Israel is our Jesus." This direct link between Israel and what Christians consider the central reality of their faith tradition obviously elicited numerous questions, most of them couched in a tone of amazement that he could make a "secular, historical" reality like Israel so pivotal for the expression of his religious belief.

The reaction of this particular audience is typical of the inability of Christians generally to grasp the role that Israel has played—and continues to play—in the self-understanding of the Jewish community. Time and time again ecclesiastical statements on Christian-Jewish relationships have omitted any reference to Israel, seeing this subject as merely political. When Jews have raised the question in a dialogue setting, uneasiness or even outright hostility has usually surfaced among the Christians in attendance. In such circumstances, the Christians have generally felt that their Jewish partners were trying to misuse theology for partisan political goals. That some Jews on occasion, particularly in very emotional settings, have given such an impression is certainly a fact. But it is impossible to exclude Israel from the dialogue agenda and hope to comprehend the uniqueness of the Jewish religious spirit. The discussion of the historic Jewish attachment to the land, because it brings into sharp focus some of the crucial differences between the two faith communities, has a rich potential for the mutual enrichment of both parties.

It needs to be made clear at this point that Christians cannot and should not justify the existence of the present State of Israel on theological grounds. The argument must be made rather on moral, cultural and political grounds. A solid case can in fact be presented for Israel on that basis. This does not exclude, however, the possibility of making a case for Palestinian rights in the current Middle East conflict. A hundred thousand theological reasons would never persuade Christians to endorse the rights of Israel to exist if its creation constituted, as it did not, a gross injustice to the other peoples in the area. On this score, Christians should reject the arguments of those Jews who would claim rights to portions of Judea and Samaria on religious grounds, as well as those of the ultra-orthodox Jews who oppose the present State of Israel because it was established by human persons rather than by the Messiah. This point needs emphasis here. For insisting on the inclusion of Israel as a major topic on the dialogue agenda does not eliminate the responsibility Christians have to retain a critical sense toward concrete policy decisions of the Israeli government.

The land tradition has been an integral part of Jewish religious self-identity since biblical times. Psalm 147, for example, speaks of the Lord rebuilding Jerusalem where the dispersed of Israel will gather, where the brokenhearted will be healed and the wounds of the suffering will be looked after. The late theologian Rabbi Abraham

Heschel, one of the giants of the twentieth-century Jewish thought, captured this traditional feeling in Judaism
in his volume *Israel: An Echo of Eternity*. As Heschel understands it, Israel, and its heart, the city of Jerusalem,
holds an almost mystical meaning for Jews:

> Jerusalem is more than a place in space . . . a
> memorial to the past. Jerusalem is a prelude, an
> anticipation of days to come. . . . It is not our
> memory, our past that ties us to the land. It is
> our future. Spiritually, I am a native of Jerusa-
> lem. I have prayed here all my life. My hopes
> have their home in these hills. . . . Jerusalem is
> never at the end of the road. She is the city
> where waiting for God was born.[110]

The dream of returning to the land of Israel gave hope to
the Jewish people during their 1900 years of enforced exile. This longing for the land was repeated each year at
the closing of the Passover Seder meal when the people
prayed, "Next year in Jerusalem."

After this Jewish hope for return to Zion entered the
realm of the possible in the latter part of the nineteenth
century, a wide body of literature flowed from Jewish
pens trying to reinterpret this hope in a modern context.
Some of the writers actually came to the conclusion that
diaspora existence, life outside the land of Israel, should
be the contemporary goal for Jews. In other words, the
traditional hope should be buried as a Jewish ideal. Many
in Reform Judaism took this position originally. Survey-
ing these various writings on Zionism, Professor Manfred
Vogel of Northwestern University has unearthed five significant strands of thought regarding Judaism's relationship to the land.[111] The first is the philosophical-religious

trend that basically tried to explain the covenant of the land in theological or philosophical categories rather than in political or ideological ones. The second is the Zionist ideological trend that clearly expressed the connection between peoplehood and land in cultural and political categories. Next we find the cultural autonomist trend which championed diaspora existence over settlement in the land of Israel. The fourth approach is the socialist one which placed a response to the question of return to the land in the context of the goals of socialism. Some socialist Jews embraced Zionism as a result with the goal of setting up socialist political structures in any new state while others felt that socialism demanded the affirmation of diaspora existence. Finally, there is the mystical trend which attempts to articulate the relationship between peoplehood and land in mystical categories.

It is not possible here to explore each of these trends in depth. Overall, Professor Vogel's research shows that the preponderance of modern Jewish formulations of self-identity do affirm the category of the land as central. And, as a result of certain events like the Nazi holocaust and the experience of the Six Day War in 1967, this affirmation has grown in recent years to the point of virtual unanimity.

There is one aspect of Professor Vogel's analysis that especially needs to be highlighted. The basic category for most of the Jewish writers on Zionism was peoplehood, not land. Essential to the notion of Jewish peoplehood was the sense of working toward redemption, of seeing the consummation of that redemption in the dimension of time. The category of land entered the structure of Jewish faith secondarily and derivatively, by what was implied in the meaning of peoplehood. In order to fulfill its redemptive vocation, the Jewish people need sovereignty—the power to regulate its life both internally and externally. Without the possession of sovereignty, the freedom to decide and direct the life of the community, the category of peoplehood cannot possibly carry out the redemptive task that is its burden.

But sovereignty can be attained only by a people in possession of a land. Thus, it should be clear that while the category of land is secondary and derived in terms of Judaism's basic faith perspective, as far as its redemptive vocation is concerned the category of land is no less essential than the category of peoplehood. Without a land to allow the exercise of sovereignty, the fulfillment (and even the very workings) of the redemptive vocation is simply impossible in Jewish eyes. Jewish faith can, and has, survived the absence of land, something it cannot accomplish without the notion of peoplehood. But this survival constituted a truncated form of existence. As Vogel puts it, "In diaspora-existence Judaism could only mark time. It could only, so to speak, hold the fort. For the resumption of the active pursuit of its redemptive vocation it had to await and hope for its restoration to the land."[112]

With the actual restoration of the State of Israel in 1948 the centuries-long yearning of the Jewish community achieved realization. As in any polyglot community, not all present-day Jews, including citizens of Israel, understand the significance of the state in the same fashion. Some view it in explicitly religious categories, as the beginning of the eschatological in-gathering of the exiles. Others see in its establishment an affirmation of life and hope after the destruction and death of the Nazi holocaust. They see it as the ultimate Jewish victory over Hitler. Professor Emil Fackenheim has said that after the experience of the holocaust the survival of Israel has become the 614th commandment of the Torah. It is the only way Jews have today of insuring that Hitler will not be granted a posthumous victory. The majority of Jews in Israel, victims of persecution in Hitler's Germany, in Arab countries, and in the Soviet Union have experienced it as a place of survival where they can enjoy a new life in dignity and freedom. But even those Israelis who choose not to interpret Israel in strictly religious terms tend, in their so-called secular language and terminology, to echo the spirit of the land tradition that permeates the Hebrew Scriptures and the rabbinic tradition.

As Christians approach the study of the land tradition in Judaism and its expression in contemporary Israel, several questions arise. Is this religious concern about the land of Israel a part of the historic Jewish commitment to salvation within history? This is what Manfred Vogel seems to imply. Is the general inability of Christians to understand the Jewish perception of the land of Israel the result of an abandonment of a sense of history by Christian theology which was discussed in Chapter Two? Has a "heavenly" Jerusalem vision emasculated Christian awareness of God's salvific action within the flow of history and in so doing made it impossible for the church to identify in a real way with the biblical spirit? What function, if any, does Israel play in Christian self-understanding today?

In dealing with these questions Christians will have to take very seriously the pioneering work of such Christian biblical scholars as W.D. Davies, John Townsend and Walter Brueggemann. While there are differences in their perspectives, they nonetheless seem to agree that (1) the New Testament does not clearly rule out Judaism's historic claim to the land; and (2) that land remains important for Christian faith, at least to the extent that the process of salvation in Christianity is deeply rooted in the process of human history.

Brueggemann is perhaps the strongest of these voices regarding the continued importance of the biblical land tradition for *both* Jews and Christians in our time. The interpretation of Scripture has thrived, he says, on the construction of antitheses between space/time and nature/history. Time and history were generally looked upon as distinctive Hebrew categories. He rejects this usual classification. In the Hebrew Scriptures we find no timeless space or spaceless time. There is rather what Brueggemann calls "storied place," a place which derives its significance from the history it has witnessed:

> There are stories which have authority because they are located in a place. This means that biblical faith cannot be presented simply as an historical movement indifferent to place which could have happend in one setting as well as another, because it is undeniably fixed in this place with this meaning. And for all its apparent "spiritualizing," the New Testament does not escape this rootage. The Christian tradition has been very clear in locating the story in Bethlehem, Nazareth, Jerusalem, and Galilee.[113]

Brueggemann insists that the antithesis of the God of history over against the gods of the land is outdated. Yahweh is both lord of historical events as well as the fructifier of the land. He is a fertility god who gives life as well as an historical god who saves and judges. He remains Lord of places as well as of times. Such an understanding raises serious questions with the existentialist approach to biblical interpretation usually associated with Rudolf Bultmann. This school of thought has exercised a strong influence in modern biblical scholarship. It mistakingly tried to free the New Testament from the biblical land tradition in favor of personal meaning for the individual believer acquired through instantaneous and radical decisions of obedience. It is obvious that such a Christian approach would have little sympathy with current Jewish reflection on the meaning of the State of Israel. Brueggemann believes such an approach must be discarded because it is unsound in view of contemporary scholarship. It is a misunderstanding of biblical categories.

The central problem for him "is not emancipation but *rootage*, not meaning but *belonging*, not separation from community but *location* within it, not isolation from others but *placement* deliberately between the generation of promise and fulfillment."[114] Both the Hebrew Scriptures and the New Testament present homelessness as the central human problem. They seek to respond to it in terms of promise and gift. Thus a truly believing Christian will need to make land a principal category in his or her belief system every bit as much as a faithful Jew.

Professor W.D. Davies of Duke University in his massive study of the land tradition entitled *The Gospel and the Land* is stronger than Brueggemann in insisting on a difference between Judaism and Christianity in this respect. Davies says that with regard to the land promises in the Hebrew Scriptures, the New Testament must be classified as ambivalent. There are strata within the New Testament that view this tradition in a critical light and one stratum (Acts 7) rejects it outright. But there are other passages in which the land, the Temple and Jerusalem, in an actual physical, not spiritual, sense are looked upon positively. They retain a significance for the Christian gospel.

As Davies sees it, then, the New Testament presents a twofold witness. On one hand, it transcends the land, Jerusalem, the Temple. Yet its history and theology cannot escape concern about these realities. In the New Testament, says Davies, holy space is to be found wherever Christ is or has been:

> It personalizes "holy space" in Christ, who, as a figure of history, is rooted in the land; he cleansed the Temple and died in Jerusalem, and lends his glory to these and to the places where he was, but, as Living Lord, he is also free to move wherever he wills. To do justice to the personalism of the New Testament, that is, to its Christocentricity, is to find the clue to the various strata of tradition that we have traced and to the attitudes they reveal: to their freedom from space and their attachment to spaces.[115]

Professor John Townsend limits his investigation to the question whether the New Testament rules out the continuation of Jewish land promises as a matter of Christian belief. Though he says that the matter is difficult to handle since the New Testament does not address it head-on, indirect references in certain parts of the New Testament do reveal attitudes which suggest a certain acceptance of the land promises as a continuing valid heritage belonging to Israel "according to the flesh." Jesus certainly acted, according to Townsend, in ways that would naturally have led his contemporaries to understand him as one who would help in fulfilling the land promises of the Jewish covenant by restoring the land fully to Israel. There is little reason in his mind to doubt that Jesus was at least partially in sympathy with such an interpretation of his message even though he never began any armed revolt as did other nationalists. But this is as far as Townsend is willing to speak on the matter. Unlike Brueggemann and Davies he is unwilling to offer any possible meaning of the land promises for Christian faith. The one thing Christians cannot do, however, is claim without qualification that the New Testament completely wipes out Jewish claims to the land after the Christ Event.[116]

In summary judgment about these three positions, we can say that they are all correct in ruling out any simple abrogation of the Jewish land tradition by the gospel message. The rootedness in history that both Brueggemann and Davies see as a primary legacy of the land tradition and a continuing need for the church today is a most welcome development. Brueggemann, however, does not seem to make enough of a distinction between Jewish and Christian understandings of the land tradition. Davies appears closer to the truth in this respect even though his formulation of the difference may require further nuancing and qualification. While Christianity would sacrifice an essential component of self-identity by dropping the land tradition from its credo, it would also lose some of its uniqueness if it were to appropriate it totally in the way Brueggemann suggests. Articulation of the difference between Judaism and Christianity on the land tradition issue needs further attention from scholars. There is need to build on the fine basis laid by the three scholars in question.

Inclusion of Israel on the dialogue agenda will prove an important learning experience for Christians. In the first place, the existence of the state can become a powerful tool in the general Christian theological effort to reexamine the meaning and destiny of the Jewish People. It can help the church realize that God did not abrogate his covenant with Israel. The Jews are still his people, beloved and cherished. God is faithful; he does not renege on promises once made.

In this connection Christians also need to ask themselves how they handle the long-standing theological tradition in Christianity that Jews were destined to be perpetual wanderers among the peoples of the earth as a punishment for murdering the Messiah. We saw in Chapter One how this theology played a key role in Catholicism's response to the rise of modern Zionism. This "perpetual wandering" theology, though definitely on the wane, raised its head again in 1948 in the Vatican's decision not to recognize the new State of Israel. The unofficial organ of the Vatican, *Osservatore Romano*, wrote the following:

> Modern Zionism is not the authentic heir of biblical Israel, but constitutes a lay state. This is why the Holy Land and its sacred places belong to Christianity, the veritable Israel.[117]

While this "perpetual wandering" theology has been largely discredited in mainline Christian circles, it is vital for Christians to know how influential it was in shaping the modern Christian outlook toward Zionism and Israel.

The second important benefit to be gained from dialogue about Israel is the improved understanding it provides Christians of Judaism's sense of salvation in a communal and historical context. Integral to the contemporary renewal of Christianity is the attempt to move away from the exclusively otherworldly, individualistic conception of redemption that has pervaded the church for so long a time. By contact with the Jewish tradition, Christians will come to appreciate more profoundly the need to express their faith within the categories of peoplehood and history. In point of fact, as Rabbi Robert Gordis has perceptively observed, the contemporary renewal process in the Christian churches may be described as the "re-Judaization" of Christianity.

The Jewish affirmation of hope and life in the face of the evil of Auschwitz that Israel represents will serve as another powerful lesson for the Christian churches throughout the world as they increasingly confront oppression and injustice. Coming to grips with the land tradition will also force Christianity to look anew at its traditional claim of "universality" and how in fact it has related that to the category of sovereignty. Do Christians also need cultural and political dominance in some areas of the world to insure the continuation of their redemptive mission in the way Professor Vogel has suggested for Judaism? Put another way, will Christianity survive if it becomes everywhere a minority? There is also need to ask whether Christian "universality" is as different from, and as superior to, Jewish "particularity" as the church has customarily argued?

On this latter question, a statement in a study guide published by the United Presbyterian Church in the USA (1973), entitled *Peoples and Conflict in the Middle East*, is very much to the point:

> Not only is Israel a reminder of the vitality of Judaism but it also reminds us of the particularism of biblical faith. We are often inclined to assume that God reveals himself through abstract

principles and universal categories. The "scandal" of particularity is manifest in Jewish identification with Israel in a way which parallels the "scandalous" claim of Christianity that the full and decisive revelation of God to man is Jesus of Nazareth.[118]

Pursuing this issue further, we need to question the historical accuracy of the basic Christian contention that it has been more universal than Judaism. Professor Jacob Neusner has challenged this claim. He insists that upon examining Christian theologies on Judaism in late antiquity, we derive an amusing irony. Proof is abundant that Christians eagerly set out to show themselves an ethnic group, a new people formed out of the people of this world into the congregation of the Lord, replacing the old congregation of Israel. In actual fact Christians east and west admired the highly ethnic character and loyalty of Jewry. The claim on the part of the church to constitute the "new Israel" was

> not merely an effort to find a share in the Hebrew Scriptures or to take over the prophecies and promises of the Jews' holy books. It was rather a very serious effort, central to Christian theology on the church itself, to demonstrate that through Christ Christians came to constitute an ethnic group, Israel, no different from the ethnic group formerly formed by Jewry.[119]

Ancient history aside, in the present day it is possible to see how the term "Jew" has produced better social integration of peoples from diverse ethnic and racial backgrounds than the term "Christian." While one could scarcely claim that perfect social harmony has existed in American or any other segment of world Jewry, including the present State of Israel, it is significant that within modern Israel where Jews from a multiplicity of countries have found a home, the general identity of these varied peoples as "Jews" has produced greater social cohesion than we have witnessed among diverse groups of people in other nations who answer to the title "Christian." "Jew" has become a primary mark of identification that has generally transcended racial and ethnic backgrounds. "Christian" on the other hand has generally served only as a secondary source of identification which has given way to racial, ethnic and nationalistic identities, especially in times of social stress. We need only look to the United States for confirmation of this, to see how little the sharing of the Christian heritage by Blacks and Hispanics has meant with regard to acceptance by their white "Christian" brothers and sisters. The tremendous population imbalance that exists between Jews and Christians in most countries of the Western world tends to reinforce the universality-particularity model.

It is high time Christians took a long, hard look at their simplistic claims about their supposed universalistic outlook. Theologically there is some validity in contrasting Judaism and Christianity through the universal-particular model—the Pauline "in Christ there is neither Jew nor Greek" contains an important religious insight—but it needs greater nuancing. Initial analysis would seem to warrant the contention that while Christianity has maintained the "universal" ideal much more than Judaism, and it is good that the ideal has been preserved, the reality of the situation is that Judaism has done a somewhat better job of overcoming tribalism than Christianity. We have discovered so very often, perhaps most dramatically in the holocaust, that tribalism still holds deep sway over the minds and hearts of supposedly "universalistic" Christians. Certainly this process in Judaism is in part the result of an almost continued Christian persecution of the Jews throughout the centuries. But the whole explanation does not lie here.

For centuries Christianity tried to impose universality upon its diverse races and nationalities. Basically this involved an imposition of Western cultures and thought patterns upon people for whom these were foreign entities. Uniformity, at least in Catholicism, was attained but not authentic universality. Since the II Vatican Council the emphasis has been dramatically reversed, especially in Africa and Asia, as the church tries to adapt to non-Western cultures and patterns of living. This attempt at indigenization has only served to uncover how superficial the assimilation of the imposed Western Christianity has really been with the cherished "universality" that many claimed, appearing only as paper thin. This "universality" has in fact done little to really alter deep-seated native tribalism.

Judaism, on the other hand, appears throughout history to have been more willing to adapt its religious practices and symbols to different cultures. It never tried to impose a "universal" (read Western) approach upon non-Western Jews in the same way that Christianity did upon non-Western churches. The end result of this has been to bring Judaism further along the path of creating true universality out of tribalism than Christianity. But because the ideal of universality is more deeply rooted in Christianity the church has the potential to catch up and even go ahead of Judaism in this regard in the foreseeable future.

Another aspect of the Jewish land tradition with important potential for dialogue reflection is that developed by Jewish mystical writers. The Jewish mystical tradition with regard to the land puts Christians in touch with the Jewish sense of the sacramentality of the earth. This contact will help the church overcome the negative attitudes toward "the earthly city" that have been so fundamental to much of Christian theology. Many of the insights of a person like the late Rav Kook, one of the modern giants in Jewish mystical thought, stand in close proximity to those held by a Christian like Teilhard de Chardin who devoted his life to trying to restore dignity to the realm of the earth.

The value of incorporating study of the Jewish land tradition in the dialogue is not restricted to Christians. It will also force Jews to become more sensitive to some of the theological outlooks that frequently play a role in a Christian's theological approach to Israel. These are outlooks which cannot be dismissed in the same fashion as the old "perpetual wandering" theology. In this connection we can point to the basic Protestant principle of God's continual judgment over history and historical institutions as well as Catholicism's rethinking of church-state relations. The latter has been particularly strong within American Catholicism and constitutes along with the document on the Church and the Jewish people the most important and unique contribution by the American Catholic Church to Vatican II. But this rethinking has also made it difficult for some Catholic theologians to fully comprehend the Jewish perspective on Israel.

The dialogue setting will likewise enable Christians to ask Jews some challenging questions about the land tradition. Among the questions that need to be asked are the following. Does the land tradition in Judaism necessarily demand perpetual Jewish sovereignty over a piece of real estate in the Middle East? Can the values that seem fundamental to the land tradition be sustained by the presence of a Jewish community in the Middle East under some political arrangement other than the nation-state? In other words, is the nation-state *de fide* in Jewish theology? Said another way: Does the land tradition rule out all possibility of Jewish entry into a regional form of government in the future should peace and trust finally come about among the peoples of the area?

Another question that must be faced is how Zionism, the contemporary expression of the land tradition, relates to the more universalistic trends found in Second Temple Judaism that seemed to modify in the eyes of certain Jewish scholars the emphasis on a particular piece of territory as the locale of God's presence. And was the "universalistic" thrust of so much of early American Judaism (and its consequent anti-Zionism) a natural development of this Second Temple tradition or an outright perversion of the authentic spirit of Judaism?

Lastly, the whole question of non-Jewish minorities in the State of Israel and how their role is understood in an essentially Jewish state has still to be handled adequately by Zionist ideology. Christians, in the light of their own reflections on the church-state issue provoked in part by II Vatican's Declaration on Religious Liberty, can profitably probe their Jewish partners on this score.

A final question that needs airing in the dialogue about the land tradition is the anti-Zionism-anti-Semitism controversy. Fr. Edward Flannery has explored this question in some depth over the last decade. In a 1969 article he expressed the firm conviction that one of the chief respositories of unconsciousness anti-Semitism (the chief form of the virus in our day) is the commitment to anti-Zionism.[120] In a more recent piece, Flannery believes that the last decade has witnessed some improvement in Christianity's appreciation of the meaning of Israel for Jews and hence a lessening of anti-Zionism. He also is ready to admit that a person can be anti-Zionist without necessarily being anti-Semitic. Yet, on the practical level, he feels that sufficient investigation will show that, in nearly all cases, "the anti-Zionist happens also to be an anti-Semite. The difficulty resides in the unconsciousness of present-day anti-Semitism. Since it is unconscious, it is necessarily denied, even by the anti-Zionist, who generally shows more of its characteristics than does the run-of-the-mill anti-Semite."[121]

The anti-Zionism-anti-Semitism will no doubt continue to cause some tension in the dialogue for some time to come. A good rule of thumb for approaching the problem might go as follows. If the critic of Israeli policy makes it clear that he/she is still committed to the survival of the state, whatever its shortcomings, then whether the criticism is valid or not, the person cannot be termed anti-Semitic. But if, as is true in many cases, a criticism of Israeli policies leaves the distinct impression that Israel has forfeited its right to exist because of some policy failures, then the criticism might with good justification be placed in the anti-Semitic category.

From the above analysis, it should be clear that the exclusion of Israel from the Jewish-Christian dialogue agenda seriously impoverishes the encounter and gives it an air of unreality. If Christians continue to insist on such an exclusion, they are asking for dialogue with an emaciated form of Judaism and depriving themselves of a deeply enriching confrontation with their own faith perspective. Tensions will surely arise as Jews and Christians debate the land tradition against the backdrop of political conflict in the Middle East. Dr. Michael Wyschogrod has offered as good a context for this discussion as anyone when he writes:

> There is no doubt that the existence of the State of Israel will continue to have profound effects on Jewish-Christian relations. In the post-holocaust period it is simply not possible for Jews to be indifferent to the security of the Jewish state. At the same time, great care must be taken that Jewish-Christian dialogue not become a replica—with the power element missing—of political and diplomatic negotiations. The encounter must remain a religious one even though neither Judaism nor Christianity (at their best) abdicates its concern with the events of history.[122]

6
Theological Perspectives on the Nazi Holocaust

No Christian scholar has spoken more forcefully of the implications of the Nazi holocaust, the murder of six million Jews and millions of other peoples by Nazi Germany, than the church historian Franklin Littell. According to him, the holocaust is something that happened to Christians as well as to Jews. He insists that the holocaust "remains the major event in the recent church—signalizing . . . the rebellion of the baptized against the Lord of History . . . Christianity itself has been 'put to the question'."[123] And from the Jewish side Rabbi Irving Greenberg has spoken of the holocaust as an "orienting event" for both Jews and Christians and as a direct refutation of much of the Enlightenment philosophy that has shaped the thought patterns of Western society.[124] The growing scholarly emphasis on the significance of the holocaust for faith and meaning in the modern world has been brought home on a popular level through the special on the holocaust broadcast by the NBC television network in the Spring of 1978.

As Christians and Jews have struggled with this ep-

ochal event, several interpretive problems have arisen.
Professor Emil Fackenheim of the University of Toronto,
for example, has warned that it is immoral to search for
meaning in the holocaust event.[125] From one perspective
he makes an important point. To make a positive affirmation about any aspect of the holocaust would be to risk
destroying all human sensibility. Yet the evil of Auschwitz cannot be ignored. There is a desperate need to confront the effects of Hitler's attempt at the "Final Solution" on the soul and spirit of the human community. To
fail in this task would be to endanger human integrity.

There has also been considerable debate among holocaust interpreters as to whether the holocaust fundamentally falls into the category of "irrational" or "rational." In the final analysis, it would seem that only an understanding of the holocaust as basically a rational event
does full justice to the monumental challenge it presents
for human self-understanding. To place the holocaust in
the category of the irrational would offer some relief for
the human spirit. Irrationality has always manifested itself in human experience. As tragic as its consequences
can be, the challenge to the overall creative and hopeful
image of the human person would not be as great if the
irrationality perspective were to be accepted.

The most striking feature of the holocaust now
emerging from the detailed studies on the manifold oper-
ations of the Nazi enterprise by such scholars as Professor Raul Hilberg[126] is the comprehensive and detailed
planning involved in its execution. Every step in the process was highly calculated by some of the best minds in
Germany. And the holocaust's roots lay in philosophies
developed by thinkers still recognized as giants of liberal
Western thought. The ideological parents of the holo-

caust represent the mainstream of Western culture, not its lunatic fringe.

Within a rationality perspective, what emerges from the holocaust is the attempt to create the highest ideal of humanity, the person truly liberated from all physical, mental and cultural deficiencies. This person was to be the universal ideal for all of humanity. To achieve this goal, all the supposed "dregs of humanity"—the Jews, the Poles, the Gypsies, the physically and mentally incapacitated—had to be eliminated as "polluters" of authentic personhood. The Nazis endeavored to bring into being the "new man" that the philosopher Nietzsche had spoken of so forcefully in the nineteeneth century.

The "Final Solution" launched by the Nazis was not aimed exclusively at the elimination of the Jews despite its deep ties to traditional Christian anti-Semitism. As the Israeli historian Uriel Tal[127] staunchly maintains, the "Final Solution" was meant to answer a universal crisis of man. It aimed at a total transformation of values. It wished to free humankind from the shackles of a God concept and its attendant notions of moral responsibility, redemption, sin and revelation. It sought to transfer theological ideas into anthropological and political concepts.

Professor Michael D. Ryan offers further confirmation of this basic thrust of Nazism in his theological analysis of Hitler's *Mein Kampf*. Hitler's "salvation history" was rooted in the myth of the Aryan race and its rise in history through the great cultures of the past and their fall by inter-marriage with the lesser race. The present age of wrong was understood as alienation from one's own racial heritage. Salvation constituted the restoration of that heritage through the national program of biological regeneration. This would result in the new age of the master race, the race of men and women who would create a new culture for the future—one that would last a thousand years. Such was Hitler's eschatology.

According to Professor Ryan, what is especially striking about this Hitlerian "salvation history" is that from beginning to end it clearly confines itself to the limits of time:

> It amounted to a resignation to the conditions of finitude, while at the same time asserting total power for itself within those conditions. This is what makes the logic of *Mein Kampf* theological. By asserting total control within the limits of finitude, Hitler deified himself and made himself into the Savior of the German people. It was in this respect that he thought of himself as the child of providence. . . .His world view amounted to the deliberate decision on the part of mass man to live within the limits of finitude without either the moral restraints or the hopes of traditional religion. . . .[128]

The Nazi conception of the holocaust makes the event a chapter in the history of civilization as such, not only a chapter in the history of the Jewish people. It represents the coming together for the first time of the power of modern technology, the skills of bureaucratic organization and the emancipation from traditional values. This combination resulted in the consciousness among the Nazis that they were free, and had the power to reshape humanity according to their own vision without any fear of a higher moral law.

The response to the Nazi period by Christian and Jewish theologians has taken several different directions. Most express the deep conviction that it is no longer possible to speak easily of God in traditional biblical and theological categories after Auschwitz.

On the Jewish side, one of the first thinkers to grapple in a radical fashion with the significance of the holocaust for an understanding of God was Professor Richard Rubenstein. In his volume *After Auschwitz* Rubenstein insists that only paganism can now guard against the transformation of the new power and creativity discovered by contemporary humanity into forms of mass destructiveness. He writes:

> I would like to offer my own confession of faith after Auschwitz. I am a pagan. To be a pagan means to find once again one's roots as a child of earth and to see one's own existence as wholly and totally an earthly existence. It means once again to understand that for mankind the true divinities are the gods of earth, not the high gods of the sky; the gods of space and place, not the gods of time; the gods of home and hearth, not the gods of wandering. . . . They (i.e., the Jewish people) have gone home. They have once again found a place of their own on this earth. That is paganism.[129]

While many Jewish scholars would reject Rubenstein's position as overly radical, he remains nonetheless an influential speaker on the holocaust in the Jewish community, and in interreligious meetings as well. To some degree he appears to have modified his position, claiming in recent public meetings that his approach has many parallels to that articulated by Rabbi Irving Greenberg.

Turning to Greenberg we find that in his discussion of the holocaust he examines three possible models for dealing with the God-human person relationship. They are the one found in the book of Job, the Suffering Servant imagery present in the book of Isaiah and the "controversy with God" approach based on Lamentations 3 which tends to dominate the writings of the holocaust novelist Elie Wiesel. Greenberg finds possibilities in all these models. Yet all need serious critiquing in the light of Auschwitz:

> ... None of these models can fully articulate the tensions of the relationship to God after the holocaust. And it will take time to develop these models. This suggests that we are entering a period of silence in theology—a silence about God that corresponds to his silence. In this silence, God may be presence and hope, but no longer the simple *Deus ex machina*.[130]

Greenberg goes on to argue that recreating human life is the fundamental religious testimony that needs to be given. In giving this testimony the human community may once again begin to find something of meaning, something of the presence of God. To create a life or to enhance its dignity is to offer the only possible effective counter-testimony to the holocaust:

> To talk of love and of a God who cares in the presence of the burning children is obscene and

incredible; to leap in and pull a child out of a pit, to clean its face and heal its body, is to make the most powerful statement—the only statement that counts.[131]

As Greenberg perceives the situation, the reborn State of Israel is for Jews today the fundamental act of life and meaning. To fail to understand this inextricable connection and response is to remain totally in the dark regarding the theological significance of Israel.

A third major spokesperson in contemporary Judaism relative to the theological impact of the holocaust is Professor Emil Fackenheim of the University of Toronto. For him Auschwitz poses serious religious problems for the Jew, and in significant ways these problems are new despite the continual Jewish awareness of evil in history. Fackenheim acknowledges that Jews may be tempted to contradict traditional Jewish assertions about God's presence in history in their search for God after the holocaust. Yet he feels that such temptations may be due to lack of an in-depth understanding of the Jewish tradition's approach to God. In the end Fackenheim seems to come down on the side of the continued validity of the traditional Jewish notion of God's presence in history despite the trauma of Auschwitz even though the religious Jew must continue to wrestle with this notion.

Fackenheim comes close to Greenberg in maintaining that Jewish survival, particularly Jewish survival in the State of Israel, has become the primary religious duty of Jews in the post-holocaust era. How to reconcile the death of so many during the Nazi era with the continued existence of God remains a many-sided mystery. He concludes by insisting:

For a Jew after Auschwitz, only one thing is
certain. He may not side with the murderers
and do what they have left undone. The religious Jew who has heard the Voice of Sinai
must continue to listen as he hears the com-
manding Voice of Auschwitz. And the secular-
ist Jew, who has all along lost Sinai and now
hears the Voice of Auschwitz, cannot abuse that
Voice as a means to destroy four thousand
years of Jewish believing testimony.[132]

Several Christian theologians have also looked at the
implications of the holocaust experience for theology
within the church. Gregory Baum is convinced that
Auschwitz forces us into a new understanding of the relationship between evil and the will of God. In light of the
holocaust experience it is no longer possible to assert that
God permits evil. Rather God must now be seen as the
personal power at work among people, summoning them
to uncover and oppose the evil in human life, to redirect
history and to transform the human community. For
Baum, "the death that destroys is never the will of God.
On the contrary God is the never-ending summons to
life."[133]

According to Baum the expression "This is God's
will" can never again be understood to mean that God
wants or even permits terrible calamities or injustices to
occur. For the person of faith, however, it can signify a
continuing trust that God will help fashion new life out
of a death experience such as Auschwitz:

Jewish men and women on the way to the exter-
mination chambers may have said to themselves
that this incomprehensible and groundless evil

was in some mysterious way God's will—in the
sense that they continued to trust in God. But
on the lips of an observer such a statement
would be a dreadful blasphemy.[134]

For Baum, we must cease explaining God's power over
the world as the miraculous action by which he makes
things happen as he chooses. Rather the only valid interpretation after the holocaust is to see it as a redemptive
action by which God enables people to deal with their
problems and by which he calls them to resist evil and
discover new ways to overcome it.

Another Christian theological perspective that has
emerged in recent years connects Jewish suffering during
the holocaust with the suffering endured by Christ. One
example of this school of thought can be found in the
writings of Professor Franklin Sherman. For him the
only legitimate way for Christians to speak about God
after Auschwitz is to recognize his participation in the
sufferings of people who in turn are called upon to take
part in the sufferings of God. Sherman writes:

For Christianity the symbol of the agonizing
God is the Cross of Christ. It is tragic that this
symbol should have become a symbol of division between Jews and Christians, for the reality to which it points is a Jewish reality as well,
the reality of suffering and martyrdom.[135]

He thus sees in the cross the revelation in the first instance of a profoundly Jewish reality. Subsequent interpretations by Christians of the sufferings of Jews must always be conscious of this Jewish reality. The God of the
post-Auschwitz age is the God who calls all people into a

new unity, not only a unity between Jews and Christians,
but one in which that unity has a very special significance.

A perspective somewhat similar to Sherman's is espoused by the Catholic Israeli writer Fr. Marcel Dubois.
He is aware of the difficulties Christians face in trying to
locate Auschwitz within a theology of the cross. He is
likewise conscious that such an association may appear to
Jews as an obscenity given the church's role in the holocaust. Yet he remains convinced that this is the direction
Christians must move in interpreting the holocaust:

> . . . In the person of the Suffering Servant there
> appears to take place an ineffable change. Our
> vision of Jewish destiny and our understanding
> of the Holocaust in particular depend on our
> compassion; the Calvary of the Jewish People,
> whose summit is the Holocaust, can help us to
> understand a little better the mystery of the
> Cross.[136]

Dubois believes that a faith perspective will allow Christians to affirm that Jesus completes Israel in her role as
the Suffering Servant and that Israel in turn, through her
experience of anguish and solitude, symbolizes, even if
unconsciously, the mystery of the passion and the cross.
Christians and Jews need to be united today in their affirmation of the fidelity of God despite the experience of
massive annihilation and in their certitude of the victory
of life over death.

There may be legitimate uneasiness among some
Christians about combining the theology of the cross
with the holocaust experience or viewing Israel as the
precursor of the sufferings of Christ. But insofar as these

interpretations stress that Auschwitz forces upon Christians a new understanding of the God-human person relationship, and insofar as they underscore that the holocaust inextricably links the fate of Jews and Christians, they help to build the foundations for a new Christian theology that still awaits full formulation.[137]

Though up till now we have stressed the implications of the holocaust experience for contemporary theological reflection, the church can never set aside the question of her failure in moral responsibility during the Nazi era. While any investigation of the root causes of the holocaust will inevitably uncover a multiplicity of factors, the words of Fr. Edward Flannery are very much to the point:

> ... In the final analysis, some degree of the charge (against the church) must be validated. Great or small, the apathy or silence was excessive. The fact remains that in the twentieth century of Christian civilization a genocide of six million innocent people was perpetrated in countries with many centuries of Christian tradition and by hands that were in many cases Christian. This fact in itself, stands, however vaguely, as an indictment of the Christian conscience. The absence of reaction by those most directly implicated in the genocide only aggravates this broader indictment.[138]

A position that the holocaust was due primarily to forces at work in modern secularism in no way exonerates the complicity of many churchpeople in the Final Solution. The architects of the holocaust found a population well primed for the acceptance of their racist theories as a re-

sult of centuries of Christian preaching and teaching
about Jews and Judaism. As Flannery puts it:

> The degraded state of the Jews, brought about
> by centuries of opprobrium and oppression,
> gave support to the invidious comparisons with
> which the racists built their theories. And in
> their evil design, they were able to draw moral
> support from traditional Christian views of
> Jews and Judaism.[139]

The lessons of the holocaust have not been studied
very deeply by Christians at large up till now. There has
been a profound fear to probe the significance of this
tragedy for Christian self-understanding. Professor Alice
Eckardt has documented the Christian reluctance to deal
with the holocaust in a survey of Christian and Jewish responses to the holocaust. The vast majority of Christians
view the holocaust as primarily a Jewish problem, whereas, in her eyes, in far deeper respects it remains a Christian problem.[140] Her findings concur with the sentiments
expressed by Professor Elwyn Smith. Smith asks:

> Was not the holocaust a terrible test—which
> the Church failed? . . . . It may be . . . that the
> question whether Christianity is to remember
> the holocaust or dismiss it is a question of the
> ability and the right of Christianity to survive in
> a form in any way conformable to the Scrip-
> tures.[141]

During the last few years a number of pioneering
Christian scholars such as Allan Davies, Gordon Zahn,

Michael Ryan and Franklin Littell have begun to probe the question in greater depth.[142] This process must continue if the Christian-Jewish dialogue is to experience a genuine growth in the future.

7
Final Reflections

From the wide-ranging number of Jewish and Christian sources dealing with the church-synagogue encounter examined in the preceding chapters it should be clear that any claim that the dialogue is dead simply ignores the facts at hand. The issues that have been highlighted will continue to occupy both Christian and Jewish scholars for decades to come. In addition to these, there are several other areas that deserve greater attention.

In the first place it is necessary to recognize that up till now the Christian-Jewish dialogue has been almost exclusively a concern of Western society. This situation has sometimes been used to try to undercut the value of the dialogue, with the implication that the remainder of the world need not bother itself with this dimension of interreligious relations. On one level it is important to recognize that the non-Western churches do not bear the historical legacy of anti-Semitism, the holocaust in particular, carried by Western Christianity. The dialogue will of necessity assume a somewhat different character in the West as a result. But since Judaism has provided the context for the very development of Christianity, no Christian church anywhere can ignore its attitudes to-

ward the Jewish people. In addition, in an interdependent
world, all nations have a stake in the current Middle East
political turmoil where religious attitudes frequently
come into play. So it is imperative that dialogue with
Jews become a deep concern of Christian churches everywhere.

African Christianity in particular has recently begun
to explore more seriously the Jewish component of Christianity. One of its prominent spokespersons the theologian John Mbiti of Kenya addressed this question during
a meeting of the World Council of Churches' Committee
on the Church and the Jewish People held in Jerusalem
in June 1977. He acknowledges that African Christianity
has been exposed to Judaism almost exclusively within
the biblical tradition. Few Africans have had living contact with Jewish people today. Two points, he feels, bring
Jews and African Christians together: God and religiosity:

> Very readily, and even uncritically, African
> Christians make or find an affinity with the
> Jewish religious heritage; and it is this, perhaps
> more than anything else, that has made it possi-
> ble for Africans to accept the Christian Faith so
> readily and quickly.[143]

Mbiti goes on to say that the Jewishness of Jesus further
enhances the close link between Jews and African Christianity.

There is also a need in the future to relate the Christian-Jewish dialogue to the wider interreligious encounter. Islam in particular needs to be brought into the conversation. The World Council of Churches has made a

beginning here through its program of Dialogue with People of Living Faiths and Ideologies. Up till now there has not been a parallel attempt to relate the various Vatican commissions dealing with interreligious concerns. While a place certainly remains for the limited Christian-Jewish conversation to continue, there is an equal need for an expanded, multi-religious discussion if we are to confront the world as it truly exists and not from a false perspective of Western dominance.

A concomitant thrust to the above must be the expansion of the interreligious dialogue, the Christian-Jewish dialogue included, from exclusive concentration on theological topics to a concern with major world social issues such as hunger, energy and warfare. Fr. Joseph Gremillion has made an excellent beginning in this direction through the recent symposia he has organized under the sponsorship of the Interreligious Peace Colloquium.[144] There is an urgent need to begin to address the fundamental global social problems from an interreligious perspective, the only perspective from which they can ultimately be addressed if religion is to make a significant contribution to the real solution of these problems. No one religion will be able to utilize its religious perspective alone in dealing with them.

Within the Western world there is a special need to use the dialogue between Christians and Jews as a way of coming to grips with the current cultural crisis. The peoples of the West are now experiencing on a mass scale an unprecedented sense of personal freedom—call it a Prometheus Unbound experience—which is leading to a rejection of imposed values from religious sources or elsewhere. Yet people are genuinely searching for values and a new spirituality. Dr. Robert Muller of the United Nations in addressing a conference on transcultural spirituality in June 1977 sponsored by the Vatican Secretariat for Non-Christians, claimed that

> the world is on the threshold of a new period in history in which our understanding and experience of spirituality catches up with the rapid pace of technology.[145]

To meet this challenge organized Judaism and Christianity will have to work together to shape the public and private values of this new society that is being born in our midst. Part of this will involve a fundamental re-examination of the legitimate role of religion in the public sphere beyond the present understanding of classic church-state separation.

It is my firm conviction that all fundamental value reconstruction in the future will need to be done at least in part in an interreligious context. For this reason, the interfaith dialogue takes on an importance far beyond the limited scope of improving Christian-Jewish relations. The Christian-Jewish encounter becomes a paradigm for the new mandate facing all Christians in our time, relating its faith perspective to the world religious traditions within the context of new value construction that will address the fundamental problems of global injustice.

Notes

1. New York: Stimulus Books, 1977.
2. New Haven: Yale University Press, 1963.
3. New York: Paulist Press, 1974.
4. New York: Paulist Press, 1973.
5. New York: Macmillan, 1965.
6. Volumes 1–4. New York: Pantheon Books, 1955, 1956, 1958, 1961: Vol. 5, *Brothers in Hope.* New York: Herder & Herder, 1970
7. New York: Holt, Rinehart & Winston, 1964.
8. New York: Seabury Press, 1974.
9. As quoted in "The Theological Dimensions of the State of Israel," paper presented to the 1970 Seton Hall University Convocation, South Orange, N.J. Also Yitzhak Minerbi, "The Vatican and Zionists: The Vatican's Attitude to Zionism up to the End of World War I," *"Immanuel,"* Vol. 1, No. 1 (Summer 1972), pp. 59–61.
10. cf. Croner, *Stepping Stones*, p. 2.
11. *Ibid.*, p. 86.
12. *Ibid.*, p. 87.
13. Portrait of the Elder Brother. New York: American Jewish Committee and the National Conference of Christians and Jews, 1972. Also cf. Franklin H. Littell, "The Strober Report," *"Journal of Ecumenical Studies,"* Vol. 9, No. 4 (Fall 1972), pp. 860–862. 1972), pp. 860–862.
14. *Faith Without Prejudice*. New York: Paulist Press, 1977.

147

15. *Jesus and the Revolutionaries*. New York: Harper & Row, 1970, p. 34.

16. *Faith Without Prejudice*, pp. 132; 135–136.

17. "The Parting of the Ways," in Lily Edelman (ed.), *Face to Face: A Primer in Dialogue*. Washington: B'nai B'rith Adult Jewish Education, 1967.

18. New York: Seabury Press, 1974.

19. Glen Rock, N.J.: Paulist Press, 1965. This is a revised edition of an earlier work by Baum entitled *The Jews and the Gospel*. Westminster, Md.: Newman Press, 1961.

20. "Are the Gospels anti-Semitic?","*Journal of Ecumenical Studies*," Vol. 5, No. 3 (Summer 1968), p. 481.

21. *Ibid.*, p. 486. cf. Heinrich Graetz, *History of the Jews*, Vol. II. Philadelphia: Jewish Publication Society, 1941, p. 237.

22. *The Gospel According to John*, Vols. 29 and 29A. Garden City, N.Y.: Doubleday, 1966, p. LXXI.

23. *Ibid.*

24. *Israel and the Church*. Richmond, Va.: John Knox Press, 1969, p. 68.

25. *Ibid.*

26. cf. "Jews and Gentiles: The Social Character of Justification in Paul," "*Journal of Ecumenical Studies,*" Vol. 5 (Spring 1968), pp. 241–267.

27. "The Apostle Paul and the Introspective Conscience of the West," "*The Harvard Theological Review,*" Vol. 56 (July 1963), p. 200.

28. "Saint Paul and the Jews," "*Engage/Social Action*," Vol. 3 (December 1976), p. 22.

29. *Faith and Fratricide*, p. 94.

30. *Ibid.*, p. 89.

31. *Ibid.*, p. 106.

32. *Ibid.*, p. 107.

33. *Ibid.*, p. 113.

34. *Ibid.*, p. 166.

35. *Ibid.*, p. 6

36. cf. "Development of the Christians' Self-understanding in the Second Part of the First Century," "*Immanuel*", No. 1 (Summer 1972), pp. 32-34.

37. cf. "The Passion According to John: Chapters 18 and 19, *"Worship,"* Vol. 49 (March 1975), pp. 130–131.

38. Institute Paper, no. 4 (Fall 1975), p. 9.

39. "Is Christianity Inherently anti-Semitic? A Critical Review of Rosemary Ruether's *"Faith and Fratricide."* *"Journal of the American Academy of Religion,"* Vol. 45 (June 1977), pp. 193–214.

40. "The Gospel of John and the Jews: The Story of a Religious Divorce." p. 21.

41. "The Pharisees in First-Century Judaism," *"The Ecumenist,"* Vol. 11 (November/December 1972), pp. 3–4.

42. For a general summary of recent Christian thinking, cf. Michael B. McGarry, C.S.P., *Christology After Auschwitz.* New York: Paulist Press, 1977.

43. "Christian Theology and the Covenant of Israel," *"Journal of Ecumenical Studies,"* Vol. 7 (Winter 1970), p. 49.

44. "Christ of the Church, not the Messiah of Israel" pp. 15–16.

45. *"Elder And Younger Brothers: The Encounter of Jews and Christians.* New York: Schocken Books, 1973, p. 142.

46. "A Response to Rabbi Olan," *"Religion in Life,"* Vol. 42 (Autumn 1973), p. 409.

47. "1948 and 1974: Trembling Journey through the Covenant," Israel Study Group, Washington, D.C., 25 October 1974, p. 44.

48. "The Resurrection and the Holocaust," Israel Study Group, New York City, 4 March 1978, p. 13.

49. "Jewish-Christian Relationship: The Two Covenants and the Dilemmas of Christology," *"Journal of Ecumenical Studies,"* Vol. 9 (Spring 1972), p. 251.

50. *Judaism and Christianity.* Chicago: University of Chicago Press, 1948, p. 30.

51. *The Foundations of Judaism and Christianity.* London: Vallentine-Mitchell, 1960, p. 131.

52. "An Invitation to Jewish-Christian Dialogue: In What Sense Can We Say That Jesus Was 'The Christ'?" *"The Ecumenist,"* Vol. 10 (January/February 1972), p. 17.

53. "Christian-Jewish Dialogue: New Interpretations," "*ADL Bulletin*," Vol. 30 (May 1973), p. 4.
54. *Faith and Fratricide*, pp. 247–248.
55. *Ibid.*, pp. 25–251.
56. Philadelphia: Fortress Press, 1977.
57. *Ibid.*, p. 552.
58. *Judaism in German Christian Theology Since 1945*. Metuchen, N.J.: The Scarecrow Press, 1975.
59. *Anti-Judaism in Christian Theology*. Philadelphia: Fortress Press, 1978.
60. Philadelphia: Westminster Press, 1968. p. 255.
61. Cf. Foreword to *The Apostle's Creed in the Light of Today's Questions*. Philadelphia: Westminster Press, 1972.
62. New York: Harper & Row, 1974, p. 132.
63. *Ibid.*, p. 134.
64. "Jurgen Moltmann, the Jewish People, and the Holocaust," "*Journal of the American Academy of Religion*, Vol. 44 (December 1976) p. 682.
65. New York: Harper & Row, 1977.
66. "Jurgen Moltmann, the Jewish People and the Holocaust," p. 689.
67. London: Collins, 1977.
68. "Is Jesus a Bond or Barrier? A Jewish-Christian Dialogue," "*Journal of Ecumenical Studies*," Vol. 14 (Summer 1977), pp. 466–483.
69. New York: Doubleday, 1977.
70. *Jesuz het Verhaal van een Leuenda* ("Jesus, the Story of One Who Lives"). Bloemendaal: Nelisson, 1974.
71. "Christology in the Jewish-Christian Encounter," "*Journal of the American Academy of Religion*, Vol. 44 (December 1976), pp. 693–703.
72. *Ibid.*, p. 701.
73. "The Myth of the Judaeo-Christian Tradition," "*Commentary*," Vol. 58 (November 1969), pp. 73–77.
74. "Judaism, Christianity and the Western Tradition," "*Commentary*," Vol. 44 (November 1967), pp. 61–70.
75. *Paul and Palestinian Judaism*, p. 548.
76. For a more detailed discussion of this point, cf. my essay "The Historicizing of the Eschatological; the Spiritualizing of the Eschatological: Some Reflec-

tions," in the critical volume under the title *Antisemitism and the Foundations of Christianity*. by Alan Davies published in 1979 by Paulist Press.

77. *"Worldwide,"* Vol. 21, (May 1978), pp. 37–41.
78. An unofficial translation of the Federici paper can be found in "Face to Face," Vol. III–IV (Fall/Winter 1977), pp. 23–31. An official translation appears in *"Origins,"* Vol. 8 (19 October 1978), pp. 273–283.
79. "Christians Challenge the Rabbi's Response, *"Worldview,"* Vol. 21 (July/August 1978) pp. 42–46.
80. cf. Walter Jacob, *Christianity Through Jewish Eyes.* Cincinnati: Hebrew Union College Press, 1974.
81. New York: Harper & Row, 1951.
82. Philadelphia: Jewish Publication Society, 1958.
83. New York: Holt, Rinehart and Winston, 1971.
84. *"The Myth of the Judaeo-Christian Tradition,"* p. 77.
85. "Judaism and Christianity—A Jewish View." *"Encounter Today,"* Vol. 7 (Summer/Autumn 1972), p. 111.
86. *"Origins,"* Vol. 6 (12 May 1977), p. 746.
87. *"CCAR Journal,"* Vol. 24 (Summer 1977), p. 72.
88. *Is Jesus a Bond or Barrier?*, p. 471.
89. *Ibid.*, p. 481.
90. "Jews and Christians in the World of Tomorrow," *"Immanuel,"* No. 6 (Spring 1976), p. 79.
91. *Ibid.*, p. 80.
92. "Towards World Community: Resources for Living Together—A Jewish view," *The Ecumenical Review*, vol. 26 (October 1974), p. 617.
93. "Cloud of Smoke, Pillar of Fire: Judaism, Christianity, and Modernity After the Holocaust," in Eva Fleischner (ed.), *Auschwitz: Beginning of a New Era?* New York: Ktav, 1977, p. 9.
94. "Facing the Truth," *"Judaism,"* Vol. 27 (Summer 1978), p. 325.
95. "Ten Years of Catholic-Jewish Relations: A Reassessment," *"Encounter Today,"* Vol. 11 (Summer/Autumn 1976), pp. 87–88.
96. "The New Encounter of Judaism and Christianity," *"Barat Review,"* Vol. 3 (June 1968), p. 121.
97. Cf. *Highlights of Proceedings of the National Confer-*

ence on Faith Without Prejudice: Religion and the Teaching of Human Relations. New York: American Jewish Committee, 1975, p. 9.

98. "Jesus in Israeli Textbooks," *"Journal of Ecumenical Studies,"* Vol. 10 (Summer 1973), pp. 515–531.

99. Cf. Helga Croner, *Stepping Stones,* p. 62.

100. *Faith Without Prejudice,* pp. 136–137.

101. *The Rabbinic Traditions About the Pharisees Before 70,* 3 vols. Leiden: N.J. Brill, 1971. For a condensed, popular summary of Neusner's research, cf. *From Politics to Piety: The Emergence of Pharisaic Judaism.* Englewood Cliffs, N.J.: Prentice-Hall, 1973.

102. *The Shaping of Jewish History.* New York: Charles Scribner's Sons, 1971: *The Hidden Revolution.* Nashville: Abingdon, 1978; "The Internal City," *"Journal for the Scientific Study of Religion,"* vol. 5 (Spring 1966), pp. 225–240; "The Pharisaic Background of Christianity," in Michael Zeik and Martin Siegel (eds.), *Root & Branch: The Jewish/Christian Dialogue.* Williston Park, N.Y.: Roth Publishing, 1973, pp. 47–70; "The Meaning of Messiah in Jewish Thought," *"Union Seminary Quarterly Review,"* Vol. 26 (Summer 1971), pp. 383–406; "Defining the Pharisees: The Tannaitic Sources," *"Hebrew Union College Annual,"* 1970, pp. 205–249.

103. Berlin: Walter De Gruyter & Co., 1961, p. 133.

104. "A New Sensitivity in Judaism and the Christian Message," Part I, *"Encounter Today,"* Vol. 4 (Autumn 1969), pp. 123–131.

105. "Defining the Pharisees," pp. 205–249.

106. "A New Sensitivity in Judaism and the Christian Message," *"Harvard Theological Review,"* Vol. 61 (April 1968), p. 126.

107. *The Foundation,* p. 137.

108. *Ibid.*

109. *Faith Without Prejudice,* pp. 133–134.

110. New York: Farrar, Straus and Giroux, 1969.

111. "The Link between People, Land and Religion in Modern Jewish Thought," *"Sidic,"* Vol. 8, No. 2 (1975), pp. 15–32.

112. Ibid., p. 29.

113. *The Land.* Philadelphia: Fortress Press, 1977, p. 185.
114. *Ibid.,* p. 187.
115. Berkeley, CA: University of California Press, 1974, p. 367.
116. "Israel's Land Promises under the New Covenant," paper presented to the Israel Study Group, 1972.
117. As quoted in Jean Paul Lictenberg, O.P., *From the First to the Last of the Just.* Jerusalem: Ecumenical Theological Research Fraternity, 1972, p. 43.
118. As quoted in Haberman, "Universalism and Particularism," p. 67.
119. "Israel and the Nations," *"CCAR Journal,"* Vol. 17 (June 1970), p. 31.
120. "Anti-Zionism and the Christian Psyche," *"Journal of Ecumenical Studies,* Vol. 6 (Spring 1969), p. 183.
121. "Zionism, the State of Israel and the Jewish-Christian Dialogue," *"Judaism,"* Vol. 27 (Summer 1978), p. 316.
122. "The Future of Jewish-Christian Relations," *"Face to Face,"* Vol. I (Winter/Spring 1976), p. 20.
123. "The Meaning of the Holocaust: A Christian Point of View," address at the University of Michigan, 3 November 1971. Also cf. Franklin Littell, "Christendom, Holocaust and Israel," *"Journal of Ecumenical Studies,"* Vol. 10 (Summer 1973), pp. 483–497 and *The Crucifixion of the Jews.* New York: Harper & Row, 1975.
124. "Cloud of Smoke, Pillar of Fire," in Eva Fleischner (ed.) *Auschwitz. . . .*
125. Cf. "The People Israel Lives," *"The Christian Century,"* Vol. 87 (6 May 1970), pp. 563–568 and *God's Presence in History.* New York: New York University Press, 1970.
126. *Destruction of the Euorpean Jews.* New York: Watts, 1966.
127. "Forms of Pesudo-Religion in the German *Kulturbereich* Prior to the Holocaust," *"Immanuel,"* No. 3 (Winter 1972), pp. 63–72.
128. "Hitler's Challenge to the Churches: A Theological-Political Analysis of *Mein Kampf,"* in Franklin A. Littell and Hubert G. Locke (eds.), *The German*

Church Struggle and the Holocaust. Detroit: Wayne State University Press, 1973.

129. "Some Perspectives on Religious Faith After Auschwitz," in Littell and Locke (eds.), *The German Church Struggle*, p. 267.

130. "Cloud of Smoke, Pillar of Fire," p. 41.

131. *Ibid.*, pp. 41–42.

132. *God's Presence in History*, p. 89.

133. *Man Becoming: God in Secular Experience.* New York: Herder & Herder, 1971, p. 245.

134. *Ibid.*, pp. 242–244.

135. "Speaking of God After Auschwitz," "*Worldview*," Vol. 17 (September 1974), p. 29.

136. "Christian Reflections on the Holocaust," "*Sidic*," Vol. 7, No. 2 (1974), p. 15.

137. For a more detailed discussion of post-holocaust Christian theology, cf. my monograph *The Challenge of the Holocaust for Christian Theology.* New York: ADL, 1978.

138. "Anti-Zionism and the Christian Psyche," pp. 174–175.

139. *Ibid.*

140. "The Holocaust: Christian and Jewish Responses," "*Journal of the American Academy of Religion*," Vol. XLII (September 1974), p. 453.

141. "The Christian Meaning of the Holocaust," "*Journal of Ecumenical Studies*," Vol. 6 (Summer 1969), pp. 421–422.

142. Cf. Alan Davies, *Anti-Semitism and the Christian Mind.* New York: Herder & Herder, 1969; Gordan Zahn, *German Catholics and Hitler's Wars;* Franklin Littell, *The Crucifixion of the Jews;* Franklin Littell and Hubert Locke (eds.), *The German Church Struggle and the Holocaust.*

143. "African Christians and the Jewish Religion," "*Christian Attitudes on Jews and Judaism*," No. 56 (October 1977), p. 4.

144. Joseph Gremillion, *Food/Energy and the Major Faiths: An Interpretative Account of the Interreligious Peace Colloquium.* Maryknoll: N.Y.: Orbis Books, 1978.

145. As quoted in the *"Newsletter"* of the American Catholic Bishops Committee for Ecumenical and Interreligious Affairs, Vol. 7 (April 1978), p. 4.

Bibliography

PREFACE AND CHAPTER 1

Markus Barth. "Was Paul an Anti-Semite?" Part II in ISRAEL AND THE CHURCH. Richmond, Va.: John Knox Press, 1969, pp. 43–78.

A leading New Testament scholar examines Paul's supposed anti-Semitism. He finds that the great Apostle is deeply imbued with the spirit and love of Judaism rather than with an out-and-out opposition to Torah.

Gregory Baum. IS THE NEW TESTAMENT ANTI-SEMITIC? New York: Paulist Press, 1965.

A leading Christian theologian's early examination of New Testament anti-Semitism. He concludes that supposed NT anti-Semitism was due primarily to the use of traditional forms of Jewish self-criticism. Baum has since changed his position in his Introduction to Rosemary Ruether's FAITH AND FRATRICIDE (see later entry) where he holds that in fact certain portions of the NT must be called anti-Semitic. Despite the change in viewpoint the volume is a good exposition of a widespread line of argument on the subject in the Christian churches.

Claire Huchet Bishop. HOW CATHOLICS LOOK AT JEWS. New York: Paulist Press, 1974.

An examination of anti-Judaic materials in Italian, Spanish and French Catholic religious textbooks.

Helga Croner (ed.). STEPPING STONES TO FURTHER

JEWISH-CHRISTIAN RELATIONS. New York: Stimulus Books, 1977.

The most comprehensive collection of key documents from Protestant and Catholic sources dealing with Christian-Jewish relations. Includes the decree of Vatican Council II on the Church and the Jewish people.

Eugene Fisher. FAITH WITHOUT PREJUDICE. New York: Paulist Press, 1977.

An update of the ground-breaking St. Louis textbook studies on Catholic-Jewish relations. The most up-to-date survey now available of Catholic teaching materials and how they handle the Jewish question.

Edward Flannery. THE ANGUISH OF THE JEWS. New York: Macmillan, 1965.

The volume that first brought the question of anti-Semitism to the widespread attention of American Catholicism. Still one of the best single-volume histories of anti-Semitism in print.

Jules Isaac. THE TEACHING OF CONTEMPT. New York: Holt, Rinehart & Winston, 1964.

The French-Jewish historian's classic examination of the roots of anti-Semitism. Isaac's writings had a profound influence on Pope John XXIII, leading the latter to give full support to Vatican Council II decree on the Jewish people.

Bernhard E. Olson. FAITH AND PREJUDICE. New Haven: Yale University Press, 1963.

The historic study of Protestant teaching materials relative to anti-Semitism.

John T. Pawlikowski, CATECHETICS AND PREJUDICE. New York: Paulist Press, 1963.

A summary and analysis of the St. Louis textbook studies on prejudice in Catholic teaching materials. Focuses in a special way on Catholic-Jewish relations.

Rosemary Ruether. FAITH AND FRATRICIDE; THE THEOLOGICAL ROOTS OF ANTI-SEMITISM. New York: Seabury Press, 1974.

An examination of the anti-Semitic origins of Christian

theology in the New Testament and the early Church Fathers. Ruether's findings of deep anti-Semitism in the classical Christian sources have been challenged by some in the dialogue. But her volume nonetheless remains central to the new discussion of anti-Semitism and Christian theology.

Samuel Sandmel. ANTI-SEMITISM IN THE NEW TESTAMENT? Philadelphia: Fortress Press, 1978.

The leading Jewish expert on the New Testament thoroughly examines the question of anti-Semitism in the NT.

Krister Stendahl. PAUL AMONG JEWS AND GENTILES. Philadelphia: Fortress Press, 1976.

A leading scholar on the New Testament and a major figure in the international Jewish-Christian dialogue examines Paul's attitude toward the Jews. Stendahl has written and spoken extensively on the subject of Christian-Jewish relations. This short volume gives some flavor of his thought.

Gerald S. Strober. PORTRAIT OF THE ELDER BROTHER. New York: American Jewish Committee and the National Council of Christians and Jews, 1972.

A brief update of how Protestant materials have improved or remained the same in their portrait of Judaism in the period since the release of Bernhard Olson's study.

Bernard D. Weinryb and Daniel Garnick. JEWISH SCHOOL TEXTBOOKS AND INTER-GROUP RELATIONS. New York: American Jewish Committee, 1965.

A summary and analysis of the Dropsie College study of prejudice in Jewish religious materials.

CHAPTER 2

A. Roy Eckardt. ELDER AND YOUNGER BROTHERS: THE ENCOUNTER OF JEWS AND CHRISTIANS. New York: Schocken Books, 1973.

One of the leading Protestant theologians in the dialogue rethinks the relationship between Judaism and Christianity. Eckardt remains one of the most prolific writers on the subject. While he has altered some of his thinking since the publication of this volume, it still remains his most comprehensive theological statement on the issue.

Tomasso Federici. "The Mission and Witness of the Church; Catholic-Jewish Relations Today," ORIGINS, Vol. 8 (October 19, 1978), pp. 273–283.

A paper delivered at an International Vatican-Jewish dialogue meeting which has elicited much discussion in dialogue circles. He argues strongly that Christians should not proselytize Jews and that the only authentic form of Christian witness to Jews is dialogue. The strongest positive statement on Catholic-Jewish relations in an official setting since Vatican II.

Eva Fleischner. JUDAISM IN GERMAN CHRISTIAN THEOLOGY SINCE 1945. Metuchen, N.J.: The Scarecrow Press, 1975.

An examination of a major source of constructive Christian theology in our time and how it has still failed to seriously deal with the Jewish question despite the horror of Auschwitz.

Charlotte Klein. ANTI-JUDAISM IN CHRISTIAN THEOLOGY. Philadelphia: Fortress Press, 1978.

A leading figure in the dialogue shows how much of contemporary Christian biblical scholarship and theology is seriously tainted by an anti-Judaic stance.

Hans Küng. ON BEING A CHRISTIAN. London: Collins, 1977, and "Is Jesus a Bond or a Barrier?" in SIGNPOSTS FOR THE FUTURE. New York: Doubleday, 1978.

A central figure in contemporary Christian theology looks at Jewish-Christian relations. The latter piece involves a dialogue between Küng and the Israeli Orthodox scholar Pinchas Lapide.

Michael B. McGarry, C.S.P. CHRISTOLOGY AFTER AUSCHWITZ. New York: Paulist Press, 1977.

A short summary with some critique of how Christian theologians have treated Christian-Jewish relations after the holocaust. Gives a good overview of current thinking even though the treatment of the respective theologians is quite brief. Needs to be supplemented with other readings.

Jurgen Moltmann. THE CRUCIFIED GOD. New York: Harper & Row, 1974.

A major Protestant theologian tries to deal constructively with the implications of the Nazi holocaust for Christian theologizing today. His sensitivity is right, though his stance still remains rather inadequate in the way it links Christianity and Judaism.

Wolfhart Pannenberg. JESUS, GOD AND MAN. Philadelphia: Westminster Press, 1968.

One of the early proponents of the new theology of hope deals extensively with Judaism in his attempt to construct a theology of Christian freedom. Despite his good intentions the volume is a continuation of many of the traditional stereotypes about the Jewish law tradition.

James Parkes. THE THEOLOGICAL FOUNDATIONS OF JUDAISM AND CHRISTIANITY. London: Vallentine-Mitchell, 1960.

One of the genuine pioneers in improved Christian-Jewish relations offers a comprehensive exposition of how the two faith communities relate to one another. He focuses his interpretation on the differing but ultimately complementary experiences of Sinai (communal) and Calvary (personal). While Parkes' thought is not the final word on the subject of Christian-Jewish relations, he made some of the early breakthroughs.

E. P. Sanders. PAUL AND PALESTINIAN JUDAISM. Philadelphia: Fortress Press, 1977.

Will likely become a classic work on the subject. The first part of the book contains one of the best and most comprehensive studies of Palestinian Judaism produced by a Christian scholar to date. Sanders sees Pauline Christianity and Palestinian Judaism as essentially different styles of being religious.

CHAPTER 3

Leo Baeck. THE ESSENCE OF JUDAISM. Philadelphia: Jewish Publication Society, 1958.

> One of the classic Jewish statements on the relationship between Judaism and Christianity. While its conception of Christianity is overly narrow, it still remains an important work in the history of Jewish thinking about Christianity.

Irving Greenberg. "Cloud of Smoke, Pillar of Fire: Judaism, Christianity, and Modernity after the Holocaust," in Eva Fleischner (ed.), AUSCHWITZ: BEGINNING OF A NEW ERA? New York: Ktav, 1977.

> A leading Jewish figure in the dialogue explains his feelings about how the holocaust has altered the shape of theological/philosophical construction in Western culture for both Christians and Jews. A powerful piece.

Walter Jacob. CHRISTIANITY THROUGH JEWISH EYES. Cincinnati: Hebrew Union College Press, 1974.

> Perhaps the best available survey of Jewish thinking about Christianity. One of its drawbacks is its lack of treatment of the Israeli scene where some interesting reflection is currently taking place.

Franz Rosenzweig. THE STAR REDEMPTION. New York: Holt, Rinehart and Winston, 1971.

> Along with Baeck's volume, the real classic in Judaism's understanding of Christianity. It will exercise far more influence in contemporary Judaism than Baeck's volume.

CHAPTER 4

David Flusser. JESUS. New York: Herder & Herder, 1969.

> One of the leading Jewish experts on the New Testament and Christianity sets Jesus within the context of Second Temple Judaism.

Jacob Neusner. THE RABBINIC TRADITIONS ABOUT THE PHARISEES BEFORE 70, 3 vols. Leiden: Brill, 1971. For a condensed, popular summary of Neusner's research, cf. FROM POLITICS TO PIETY: THE EMERGENCE OF PHARISAIC JUDAISM. Englewood Cliffs, N.J.: Prentice-Hall, 1973.

Neusner is probably the best known interpreter of the Pharisaic movement today. He has tried to apply the tools of modern biblical scholarship to the Pharisaic materials. He has serious disagreements with Rivkin's approach (cf. below) as Rivkin does with him. But Neusner and Rivkin agree on many points. They are two of the leading expositors of the Pharisaic tradition in our time.

Ellis Rivkin. THE SHAPING OF JEWISH HISTORY. New York: Charles Scribner's Sons, 1971, and THE HIDDEN REVOLUTION. Nashville: Abingdon, 1978.

See above. Rivkin approaches the Pharisaic materials with the tools of the professional historian rather than the biblical scholar.

Paul Winter. ON THE TRIAL OF JSSUS. Berlin: Walter De Gruyter & Co., 1961.

An interpretation of Jesus in the light of Second Temple Judaism that sees him as very much a part of the Pharisaic movement.

CHAPTER 5

Walter Brueggemann. THE LAND. Philadelphia: Fortress Press, 1977.

An excellent introduction to the meaning of the Jewish land tradition and its implications for the dialogue.

W. D. Davies. THE GOSPEL AND THE LAND. Berkeley, CAL.: University of California Press, 1974.

Perhaps the most thorough study of the Jewish land tradition and its implications for Christianity from the standpoint of Christian scholarship. Davies and Brueggemann would have some disagreements between them, but they are the two best Christian sources currently available.

Abraham J. Heschel. ISRAEL: AN ECHO OF ETERNITY. New York: Farrar, Strauss and Giroux, 1969.

One of Judaism's most famous and sensitive theologians gives a somewhat personal exposition of what the land means for the Jewish tradition.

CHAPTER 6

Lucy Davidowicz. THE WAR AGAINST THE JEWS. New York: Holt, Rinehart & Winston, 1978.

The major work on the holocaust by one of its leading Jewish commentators.

Emil Fackenheim. GOD'S PRESENCE IN HISTORY. New York: New York University Press, 1970.

One of Judaism's outstanding contemporary thinkers turns his attention to the meaning of the holocaust for contemporary Jewish faith.

Eva Fleischner (ed.). AUSCHWITZ: BEGINNING OF A NEW ERA? New York: Ktav, 1977.

A score of distinguished Jewish and Christian scholars focus on the significance of the holocaust. One of the best collections of holocaust essays currently in print.

Raul Hilberg. THE DESTRUCTION OF THE EUROPEAN JEWS. New York: Watts, 1966.

One of the classic studies on the Nazi era. Hilberg penetrates the meaning and efficiency of the Nazi system. A crucial book for any proper understanding of the holocaust.

Nora Levin. THE HOLOCAUST. New York: Schocken Books, 1973.

Another important interpretation of the holocaust.

Franklin Littell. THE CRUCIFIXION OF THE JEWS. New York: Harper & Row, 1975.

One of the foremost Christian interpreters of the holocaust shows how classical Christian hatred of the Jews culminated in the Nazi era.

F. Littell and H. Locke (eds.). THE GERMAN CHURCH STRUGGLE AND THE HOLOCAUST. Detroit: Wayne State University Press, 1974.

One of the best collections of essays on Christian involvement in the holocaust and its significance for the future of the Church.

John T. Pawlikowski, THE CHALLENGE OF THE HOLOCAUST FOR CHRISTIAN THEOLOGY. New York: Anti-Defamation League, 1978.

An attempt to spell out the theological implications of the holocaust for contemporary Christian belief.

69854

Other Books in This Series

WHAT ARE THEY SAYING ABOUT JESUS? by
Gerald O'Collins, S.J. $1.95
WHAT ARE THEY SAYING ABOUT THE RESUR-
RECTION? by Gerald O'Collins, S.J. $1.95
WHAT ARE THEY SAYING ABOUT THE BOOK
OF REVELATION? by John J. Pilch $1.95
WHAT ARE THEY SAYING ABOUT DOGMA? by
William E. Reiser, S.J. $1.95
WHAT ARE THEY SAYING ABOUT THE TRIN-
ITY? by Joseph A. Bracken, S.J. $1.95
WHAT ARE THEY SAYING ABOUT DEATH AND
CHRISTIAN HOPE?   by   Monika   K.   Hell-
wig $1.95
WHAT ARE THEY SAYING ABOUT LUKE AND
ACTS? by Robert J. Karris, O.F.M. $1.95

From your bookstore or from
Paulist Press
545 Island Road
Ramsey, N.J. 07446